KU-505-181

Chakras, Yoga & Consciousness

Balancing Your Life

Werner Bohm

SAMUEL WEISER, INC.

York Beach, Maine

First published in 1998 by
Samuel Weiser, Inc.
P. O. Box 612
York Beach, ME 03910-0612

English translation copyright © 1991 Samuel Weiser, Inc.
All rights reserved. No part of this publication may be reproduced or transmitted in any form or by any means, electronic or mechanical, including photocopying, recording, or by any information storage and retrieval system, without permission in writing from Samuel Weiser, Inc. Reviewers may quote brief passages. First published in German as *Die Wurzeln der Kraft Chakras—die Kraft de Lotosblumen*. Copyright © Scherz Verlag, Bern-Munchen-Wein (for Otto Wilhelm Barth Verlag).

Library of Congress Cataloging-in-Publication Data

Bohm, Werner.
    [Wurzeln der Kraft Chakraas.   English]
    Chakraes, yoga & consciousness.
      p.   cm.
    Originally published: Chakras, roots of power, 1991.
    ISBN 1-57863-041-X (alk. paper)
    1. Chakras—Miscellanea.   I. Title.
    [BF1442.C53B6413   1998]
    131—dc21   97-32879
                                        CIP

BJ

Cover painting is titled "Fire over Earth," from *Images of the I Ching* (Roseville, NSW, Australia: Craftsman House, 1987), © 1991 Ann Williams. Used by kind permission of the artist.

Translated by Transcript, Ltd., Wales
Typeset in 11 point Galliard

Printed in the United States of America
06   05   04   03   02   01   00   99   98
10 9 8 7 6 5 4 3 2 1

The paper used in this publication meets the minimum requirements of the American National Standard for Permanence of Paper of Printed Library Materials Z39.48-1984.

Table of Contents

Foreword

That "books have their fates" has been much quoted—usually in allusion to the neglect a book can suffer after initial fame or notoriety before being rediscovered.[1] Indeed there are many turns and twists of fortune awaiting books and their authors. But, in another sense, the words aptly describe the way in which truly seminal works seem destined to appear when they are needed. If one has an eye for the deeper, evolutionary, spiritual requirements of a specific, often quite brief, span in the life of a few generations, we find that the appearance of an important book is not decided by the author or publisher. It has to wait until the time is ripe before it can come out. Many authors have an instinct about the right moment for their books to be published, and may even arrange for this to be done some time after their deaths: the best known example is Goethe's *Faust, Part II*. There are books in which the Spirit of the Age is at work, even to the point of deciding the year of their birth.

Werner Bohm's study of the lotuses (chakras) is without doubt one of those books that are called forth by the Spirit of the Age, their year of publication being neither arbitrary nor accidental. As it happens, I can vouch for the fact that all the things in it were envisaged by the author years before he

---

[1] "Habent sua fata libelli." Terentianus Maurus. *Tr.*

expressed them in literary form, because he kindly shared them with me in a series of charming letters. Actually, the letters are more detailed and elaborate than the present work. Today the supplementary material is no longer required as it was some ten years ago. This bears out what I was saying about the fate of a book being decided by an influence other than that of author or publisher. The ripeness of the time is seen in the fact that the book answers a deep and widespread need. What is more, the book will be discovered accidentally by many of those for whom it is intended.

Much has already been written in the West (and even more in the East) on the subject treated in this book—the chakras or lotuses, the force centers of the human being. But what has so far been published is partly just a record of Indological or Sinological research and partly the more or less harmless hokum served up by pseudo-occultists with a pretentious air of mystery. In addition, there are a few rare manuscripts that never come on the market but circulate among the members of very private groups. These manuscripts are usually illustrative teaching material that has grown out of the work of a master with his pupils, notes that are full of signs, symbols, cryptic expressions, and nomenclature. It is not by design, but in the nature of the case, that these manuscripts are incomprehensible to outsiders. And so these things are hidden from the uninitiated as long as the knowledge of them must remain esoteric on evolutionary grounds. The Spirit of the Age decides the moment when the veil is to be removed and the esoteric is to be made exoteric.

This I believe is how we should view Werner Bohm's book. So far, publications on the chakras have apparently had to remain unintelligible in the West, and Bohm's book appeals to me as being the first successful attempt to present the nature and functions of the chakras to Western minds in a form that can be accepted and assimilated. The fact that it is being placed in our hands now is certainly not accidental.

An interest in the chakras will also elaborate several alternative therapies that Westerners are just beginning to explore. As we all know, zone therapy holds an important place in alternative Western medicine. For example, it was the basis of the celebrated connective tissue massage employed in Europe by Frau Dicke of Bodensee. It was preceded by the equally successful Swedish point-massage. There has also been a resurgence of interest in the ancient Chinese practice of acupuncture (acus = a needle, punctura = a prick), associated with the ancient Chinese and Indian pulse diagnosis. In France, this therapy was studied longer and more thoroughly than in Germany, and the French developed very specific acupuncture techniques. It was the Dutch physician Ten Rhyn who first introduced acupuncture to France via Brussels at the end of the 17th century. It was becoming increasingly popular among doctors, when its rather indiscriminate use in the days of the French Revolution brought it into discredit. In Napoleonic times it was a favorite object of ridicule in cartoons. With the advent of chemotherapy, acupuncture fell into almost complete abeyance. In 1824 a book on acupuncture by the Englishman, Churchill, was translated into German, and with that this therapy became known to a wider circle in Germany.

Acupuncture is a method of healing illnesses by sticking golden, silver and gray needles into very precisely located points projected onto the body's surface. This method has been part of Chinese medicine for about four thousand years. In China, acupuncture was based on an assumption that life forces are continually streaming through the living body, and that these life forces have different power centers in the human being. These centers are, in fact, the lotuses or chakras. Bohm accurately describes and names these centers in the book now in your hands. According to the Chinese, the life force, often called prana in India, flows in invisible channels. These also appear on the surface of the skin, which they even cut in a few places when the life forces flow clear of the skin in their channels. The Chinese give the name meridians to the course of the life force below the surface of the body and on the skin. We distinguish twelve classical meridians and some minor ones. The needles are inserted a few millimeters deep into the skin at topographically exact locations. In general, it can be said that acupuncture therapy regulates the life energy (in Hindu, prana). Like the zones in zone therapy, these very precisely arranged meridians and their points correspond to definite organs and organic functions.

According to the Chinese, each of the large organs (for which the meridians are named) is associated with three points of great significance: the first point is for tonifying the organ concerned; the second for sedating it by distributing the life force; the third is known to French acupuncturists as the "source point" because the functions of the two other points depend on it. The Chinese stimulate the function from this third point, and also regulate it from here. Chinese acupuncture must not be separated from the Chinese concept of the world, and cannot be understood if you do not know the oriental metaphysics involved.

A further connection between Bohm's chakras and acu-puncture lore is the Chinese belief in the two ultimate polar principles *yang* and *yin*, which are constantly changing from one into the other. Everything else exists on account of this change. This change is subject to the Tao. Inevitably, the yang-yin philosophy also underlies acupuncture. We read in the *Li Chi* (the Chinese book of morality) that humankind contains both the spiritual forces of heaven (yang) and earth (yin), and the principles of light (yang) and darkness (yin) offset one another. In each human being the spirits and gods meet; and within us are the finest forces of the five states of change (elements). Therefore we are the heart of heaven and earth and the seed of the five states of change.

And so, there are yang organs and their above-mentioned yang meridians, and yin organs with yin meridians. The yang organs, for example, convert the food into life-building forces. The yin organs purify and store the formative forces. In Chinese thought, the essence of a disease is an imbalance in the forces of yang and yin. Acupuncture restores the balance; for example, an organ suffering from a deficiency of yang is strengthened by the insertion of the golden yang needle into the tonification point. That things are not always so simple is seen in the treatment of the so-called coupled organs (such as the liver and the gall bladder), when these diverge in yang and yin theory. The meridians are the paths of the life forces. Experience teaches that a sore place on the skin may point to a disorder in the organ the meridian of which passes through that particular spot. French acupuncturists take the Chinese view that the skin is a "representational organ of the vegetative system."

There is also a truly amazing relationship between homeopathy and acupuncture. The latest European holistic ideas hark back to the age-old Chinese doctrine of acupuncture as expressed in the following wonderful classical saying: "In choosing the right points to treat, each individual is ill in his or her own style, and this style has to be taken into account." Thus the patient is to be thought of as a unique person, and the disease is not a separate entity in its own right.

In acupuncture therapy, needles of a red metal such as gold or copper are used for tonification (yang). Needles of a white metal, e.g. silver, are used for sedation (yin). Needles of a gray metal, such as platinum, iron and steel, are neutral. This is in agreement with the tonification produced by gold salts and the cooling effect of colloidal silver in inflammation and fever. In electrochemistry the anode is gold.

In publications of the American physician Dr. Manfred Curry (who died Feb. 13, 1953), tests are described that he conducted in collaboration with the well-known German acupuncturist, Dr. Gerhard Bachmann, in Munich. Both doctors were able to demonstrate that gold needles extend and silver needles shorten the individual human reaction bands and that there was a fairly enduring effect in the patients treated. Dr. Curry writes in his report, "This is a clear indication that W-types should be treated with gold needles and K-types with silver. The results are reasons for thinking about the use of gold and silver in dentistry." What Dr. Curry and Dr. Bachmann term the individual reaction bands is a demonstrable field of energy outside the physical body, the result of something radiating from the body itself. It has been shown that the width of the reaction band depends on body shape and on the organs concerned, and that it varies in disease and in functional disorders. Without exaggeration, we can say that this is the so-called aura that surrounds every living body. The reaction band limit is the edge of the aura. Since this band has been consistently found in many thousands of controlled tests, we may regard its identification with the aura as correct. Could there be better proof that the present book by Werner Bohm has appeared at exactly the right time, that medical doctors are demonstrating the existence of the aura and are studying its origin and fluctuations?

If in this foreword to Werner Bohm's book I am talking about acupuncture, it is because the topic is so closely related to that of the chakras. In Asia, I was always encountering such connections. The concept of the chakras is not confined to India, Indo-China, China and Japan. Also, acupuncture is not restricted to China, although its first known mention is in an edict of the Emperor Huang Ti (ca. 2650 B.C.). It is easy to show that even in stone-age China, at a still earlier date, needles made of stone were being used on the human body. Acupuncture was also employed by the natives of Polynesia for as long as they preserved their stone-age culture or, in other words, before the coming of the white man (in A.D. 1777). To people at earlier cultural stages, the chakras as centers and organs of life's formative forces were as self-evident as the acupuncture points and meridians radiating these forces. Our present task is to recover their awareness. We have good grounds for assuming that we have already penetrated more deeply into the region of human, terrestrial, and cosmic formative forces and their effects than even the researchers and therapists themselves suppose. A proper awareness of these concepts will probably elude us in the West as long as we keep trying—often with increasing desperation—to understand in terms of scientific materialism the human being and the human life forces to which the chakras belong.

—Dr. Hans-Hasso von Veltheim-Ostrau

PART ONE

YOGA AND CONSCIOUSNESS

Introduction

It may seem to many readers that the state of consciousness in our times is not adapted to handling anything derived from the old doctrines of yoga. However, we modern people have been ushered into a distinctly "nervous period" in history by our inventions. Where today can we find peace and quiet? Life, especially in the West, is wearying to the soul. External sense impressions assail us in such quick succession that it is impossible to find time to assimilate them internally. The inner being is not made to cope with such a bombardment from outside. The demands made on the vegetative nervous system are too great; the tempo of life is too fast. Consequently, we have seen a rise in stress, circulatory disorders and nervous diseases. Our inner rhythmic processes cannot keep in step with the speed of external events.

Technical discoveries have tended to alienate us from ourselves. Passive behavior is forced on us by radio, television and film. We turn to them for relaxation and amusement, but they continue the bombardment our senses have been suffering throughout the day. Even sleep is restless and does not bring a natural recruitment of our forces. The struggle for existence prevents many from retiring to the peace of nature. But, in any case, where is this peace?

Nearly everywhere our world is full of the sound of engines. Planes dart through the sky at speeds greater than that of sound; cars and motorcycles race over the surface of the earth, motor boats chug along our waterways. The rattle of trucks and tractors disturbs the smallest town. Holiday resorts are full of hustle and bustle. Stimulated nerves are constantly crying out for new stimulation, and these impinge on them via the sense organs with excessive rapidity. To make matters worse, people have forgotten how to sit down and read a book that could give them intellectual and/or spiritual nourishment. People can't read anymore; they just want to look at pictures, as is demonstrated by the proliferation of picture magazines. In a way, our modern civilization is beginning to promote illiteracy!

Human intelligence and the intellect has transformed the environment in this century to such an extent that it is now having an injurious effect on body and soul. But it would be absurd to do away with the intellect. The mind has developed over thousands of years and is not yet at the end of its possibilities. It can be used in the process of inner illumination. The knowledge we Westerners are using so far is mainly concerned with physics and material sciences—everything that is most dead in the world. Up to now, the intellect has not discovered the deepest secret of matter, if it had we would know what matter really is. Although the question as to the nature of life still awaits a full and satisfactory answer, our mental abilities may not be capable of dealing with that answer.

The "central point" of our thinking needs to be released from the region of dead abstractions in which the concrete lifeforce has been trapped. Life can be comprehended only through development. Life is supersensual. When we are able to lift our awareness from the level of intellectual thought and place it on the level of spiritual thought, we shall gradually see—from the overview of spirit—the laws that operate so differently in living substance than they do in dead matter.

People often talk about a "transitional age," but development never stops.

Everywhere we look today we are confronted by "nothing," by vast emptiness. The world of the ancients was filled with gods, angels, elementals and demons. We lived with them, saw them, and received their revelations, commands and instructions. Today, the macrocosmic world is void of gods. People no longer come in contact with supernatural beings who might be able to direct and help them. This change came about as thinking turned autonomous and abstracted itself from other functions of the soul. Modern men and women seem to be thrown back on their own resources; the divine world has disappeared for them. People regard themselves as independent beings. Instead of the two Tables of the Law given on Mt. Sinai, people have provided themselves with shelves of legal volumes. We make our own laws for ourselves. The intellect appears to fragment everything. It complicates and recomplicates basic simplicity. With the hammer of our minds modern people have smashed the carefully preserved order of the ancient cosmos.

Many religious people still carry in their hearts the certainty of a divine world that is not perceptible to the normal senses. Yet are not these souls divided to the extent that they are forced to live in and conform to modern civilization? Admittedly, prayer makes it possible to make contact with the divine world. In prayer many people find the strength required for daily living. However many others make do without this basic act of faith because their intellectualism has overpowered it.

In contemporary yoga we can again find a way to link the human spirit with the reality of the supernatural divine world and turn blind faith into living experience. While traditional prayer is fairly subjective, the world to which meditation leads is more objective. Meditation is able to provide knowledge that, like scientific knowledge, is universally valid. The Spirit of the Age requires that ordinary science shall be supplemented by a spiritual science that will unlock the door to the supersensual world to which people had free access in olden times.

This supersensual world contains, naturally enough, the things that are supersensual within each of us, parts of ourselves that have lain dormant for centuries. Among these supersensual things is the lotus system, or chakras, as contemplated in the study of yoga.

The oldest Indian culture was written about in the Vedas, after previously being handed down by oral transmission. Vedanta philosophy changed its character over the years, and out of this, finally, developed yoga. Yoga reached a high water mark at the time of Patanjali. His system is a criterion for all later forms of yoga. The best-known textbook is his *Yoga Sutras.*[1]

Yoga is fundamentally important for later Buddhism, but we should go astray in this book if we tried to equate the two paths. What yoga and Buddhism have in common is a way of concentration and meditation. This is what leads to supernatural knowledge and heightened abilities. In yoga, as in Buddhism, we learn varied stages of consciousness. Like a ladder they take us, step by step, to the high places of the spirit. Philosophy, on the other hand, settles on a single step, which is normally reached straightaway.

The spiritual climate of ancient India was well suited to the meditative production and experience of different degrees of consciousness, but these experiences are open to us, too. The evidence for this can be found within. At first, it seems as if we are dealing with something that lies in the sphere of our personal subjectivity, but the impression is only partly correct because, when meditating properly, yoga aspirants can soar to regions of consciousness beyond the subjective and purely

---

[1] The date of Patanjali's birth is uncertain. Some say he flourished around 200 B.C., others suggest that A.D. 300 is more likely.

personal. We can ascend to a spiritual plane from which the subjective itself issues, and can thus attain an objective spiritual experience that is valid for all.

Western science excludes everything subjective from its research. It constructs apparatus that does not rely on the fallible human senses. Science is mechanically forced, by what lies outside us, to reach exact conclusions. This process by no means excludes the risk of error in the thought processes that are brought to bear on the results of these laboratory experiments in an endeavor to turn them into knowledge.

The path of the spiritual scholar is different. We start with the person inside the body. It is the so-called Fall, and the capacity for sinning, that have introduced error into the world within. The soul is polluted and is full of dark specters. In yoga, impossible though it may seem, an attempt is made to exclude error from the thought-life, in order to think objectively. A thorough purging of the whole individual is required in respect to the entire psychic structure. Because thinking, feeling and willing interpenetrate one another, it is of little use to clarify and cleanse the thoughts if, from the dark sphere of the will, impulses arise that make them dirty again. In the subconscious resides everything that darkens the human soul as a result of the Fall. Error, folly, delusion, the source of mischief, everything impure and impermanent, the substitution of the outer self for the true, spiritual, eternal self—all these things spring up together in the unconscious and spread their influence from there. This is the unrecognized cause of suffering and death. What is meant by the conquest of suffering is the germination of the seed of knowledge in the land of suffering and death. When our spirit penetrates to their cause, their conquest becomes a possibility. With the light of knowledge it illuminates the inner darkness.

The word yoga is similar to the English word yoke, meaning part of the harness of draught-animals. Yoga means harness, and the yogi learns to harness everything in the human soul that is animal-like—desire and the various passions. He or she learns to bring them increasingly under control, so that these lower regions of the soul obey the true self. In Greek mythology, which was contemporary with the development of yoga, we read of divine beings who taught people to bridle, drive and ride horses. The yoga aspirant will turn the physical vehicle into a spiritual temple and consecrate it to the service of the true divine world.

A modern investigator, Avalon, gives the following definition in his book *The Serpent Power*: "Yoga has been described to be the union of the individual spirit with God."[2] Rudolf Steiner who, in his work *Knowledge of the Higher Worlds and its Attainment,* discusses the lotuses and their development, and said that Yoga really meant the striving for union with divine truth.[3] (The terms "kundalini fire" and "kundalini light" employed in older German editions of this book were later replaced by words like the power of spiritual perception and spiritual light organ).

Yoga attempts to restore contact between the human spirit and the divine spirit, after the gradual loss of the direct union of the two in the era known as the "little Kali Yuga." This era is reckoned from 3101 B.C. through A.D. 1899. It brought the development of the human intellect to the pitch of being able to formulate the modern scientific method. Around 3000 B.C., we crossed the boundary between the prehistoric and the historic. Karl Jaspers calls this a leap into history. He said we could regard this leap as the ruination of mankind. On the other hand, he is willing to consider the other possibility: that this leap is the great advantage of being human, a way to undreamed-of experiences urged on by our high destiny.[4]

---

[2] Arthur Avalon, *The Serpent Power* (New York: Dover, 1974; Madras, India: Ganesh & Co., 1918), p. 181.

[3] Rudolf Steiner, *Knowledge of the Higher Worlds and Its Attainment* (Hudson, NY: Anthroposophic Press, 1947).

[4] Karl Jaspers, *The Origin and Goal of History*, trans. Michael Bullock (Westport, CT: Greenwood Press, 1977).

This was also the time that writing was invented. Its invention can be seen to push us into a new region of consciousness, where we have a greater measure of freedom and independence. Once this leap into history, this leap into the age of intellect had taken place, it was impossible to turn back. We cannot return to the former state of consciousness however much we might like to do so. The only way is forward, and our true development can come only by raising ordinary waking consciousness to a higher spiritual level, on which the lost soul asks for admittance at the long-closed door to the spiritual world. No cherub bars the way now! The Kali Yuga is over.[5]

The Yogic path is eightfold, although it is not identical with the eightfold path of Buddhism. There are difficult preconditions to fulfill, however: which are mentioned, not to place a stumbling block in the way of students, but to prepare us for things as they are. The transcendental is not accessible by pure mental activity. The will and the emotions need to be cleansed by the kind of catharsis and purification that all religions have demanded in every era.

Three components of our being, which together give us our physical existence, have to be trained until they obey the spirit, manas, or "I am." The lowest of these is the physical body, then come the life processes that penetrate it—chiefly the respiratory and circulatory rhythms. The energies in the living creature produce their own system of formative forces. These two are penetrated in their turn by sensations, the material basis of which is the nervous system. Sensation builds an organization, a "body" known as the astral body. Some sensations are physical; some are moral. In the sensations lives the soul.

The lower sensations have to do with the body; the spirit shines in the higher, moral sensations or feelings. Thus the soul

---

[5] The reference to a cherub is presumably because the trend of the author's thought has reminded him of the cherubim placed at the east of the garden of Eden after Adam and Eve had been expelled (Genesis 3:24). The Kali Yuga, Indian chronology, is the present age of conflict and sin. *Tr.*

is a link between spirit and body. It conveys the spiritual to the physical, and, on the other hand, transmits to the spirit the experiences that are open only to the earthly. Within feelings and sensations we need to find the dividing line between the animated physical world and the psychic world. One part of the soul's organism immerses itself in the physical world, while the other part soars above it. In the same way, the spirit partly irradiates the world of the soul and partly produces a separate world of its own. And so our world is made of three things, one inside another. Only one of these is spatial. Our construction is the same.

Death dismisses the three worlds found in each of us to its place of origin. For the body, this means "ashes to ashes" when life withdraws and melts into the cosmos. The feelings return to the astral plane. The individual spirit journeys back through successive spheres of the objective psychic world to the timeless spirit world, bearing life's fruits to the place from whence it came. And, if it possesses that continuous consciousness that does away with the cesuras of birth and death, it will also escape the Wheel of Rebirth for the far future.

It is natural for initiates to anticipate and personally experience stages in human development that are yet to come. Not with any selfish aim, but knowing that not only the individual but humanity need to be rescued. What initiates discover ahead of time is gradually revealed to other members of the human family, for initiates become helpers and teachers. Actually, the term initiate is very broad, because initiation starts with the study of the supernatural, and takes many forms along the way.

When thinking, feeling and willing have been purified, and the dark places of the soul have become light, communion with the divine spirit is possible. The sphere has been reached from which originates the impulse behind each "becoming," each act of creation. The spirit is always primary. The spiritual Word, or Logos, is creative. Setting out from the spiritual impulse, the spiritual will penetrates the regions of light, life, feeling, until it condenses physically and enters matter in a spiritual form. The spirit is universally creative.

The Western World cannot cope with this body-soul problem; we know that the process can begin in the mind and end in the body, but not how. The West speaks of stimulatory substances formed out of hormones, ferments and vitamins, which act on a responsive substrate, the complex protoplasm of the cells (Alexander von Papp). It speaks of "doors to a world that stretches from heavenly delight to hellish torment."

Westerners, with all their knowledge, still don't understand the knowledge that can be found in yoga, that the spiritual enters stage by stage from the world of non-form (Arupa) through the world of abstract form (Rupa) and the world of the senses (the astral) into the systems of living formative forces (the life body) from which it fashions the physical. To modern scientists, the world comes out of "nothing." However, this "nothing" of the modern scientists exists as spiritual will, will-substance, energy. People today are doing things the wrong way round by operating on the life of the soul with drugs (truth drugs, for example) and other substances; assaulting it with dark matter and its demons! Most scientists are largely ignorant of the forces they have unleashed to destroy the soul and the human image. Unaware, they are descending into the realm of black magic!

It was once an esoteric secret that to whatever extent the gates of the paradisiacal divine world open, so do the gates of Hell. No one is subject to greater temptation than the one who, with devotion and adoration, begins to catch sight of higher worlds. For this reason, neophytes used to be put through tests of courage before being allowed to proceed.

From what has already been said, it will be clear that technical devices or products cannot lead to higher knowledge or abilities. The Kingdom of Heaven is not entered by doing simple breathing exercises or by adopting a special diet—even if it is a vegetarian diet. Nor is it obtained by such artificial means as outward asceticism or by retreating from the world. The way is hard, because it demands much more than most people are usually ready to give. The difficulty lies in attaining to the spiritual level, and the spiritual world is eminently moral.

In the following chapters I will explain the way to set forth and how the stages of yoga follow one another.

The Eightfold Path
of Yoga

According to the Yogasutra of Patanjali, the yoga path leads upward in eight stages. Before going into an explanation of the chakras, we need to discuss the various stages of this path.

First Stage (Yama)

The first stage is the ethical basis of the teaching. Yama is also the name of the Indian god of death, who instructs in the secrets of yoga. Possibly this name was chosen as the designation of the first rung on the ladder of yogic doctrine because this is where we learn that knowledge and death are related. Knowledge grows out of suffering. Death is the greatest suffering of ordinary human beings, so it is from death that the highest knowledge may be expected. When people die, they are born into the psychical-spiritual cosmos. And, vice versa, birth on earth is a death in the sphere of the spirit. Now, for those who are starting out on the path, this is a revolutionary concept!

Death removes the hindrances that separate us from the divine world. Death should not be feared but recognized for what it is. Each advance in knowledge removes hindrances from the soul and spirit; when we learn something new something old has to die. This is where death becomes a friend. By correct and profound meditation we pass permanently through what the "profane" can only experience in death itself: we come to union with the truth, to communion with the divine world. In pre-Christian initiations—those of ancient Egypt, for instance—neophytes were thrown into a deathlike sleep, in which the priest and his assistants were able to make the soul and certain of the life forces leave the inert body. The neophytes then experienced the macrocosmic world with its secrets. After three days, the soul was restored to the body in such a way that the initiates retained the memory of this spiritual voyage of discovery. Now they were initiates.

Today this is no longer possible. On the yoga path, students have to rely on themselves. A guru (teacher) can only give advice. Nevertheless, the world changes at the very first stage. We come more and more to our senses, to what subsists in our innermost being. Obviously, there must be a readiness to let go of ingrained concepts in order to build anew. We have allowed our current civilization to push us into a dead end, and we must be prepared to become more fluid in our thinking.

At stage one, moral purification is needed. This is by way of preparation. After all, we go to a wedding in festive attire. Since it is the soul that is being invited to a wedding, the soul has to be clean and "dressed" for the occasion. One concept that is given a new meaning is that of ownership. If we wish to obtain something from the divine world, we must be capable of becoming completely free from possessions. I am not saying that we can possess "nothing," but that we must be prepared to part with possessions at any time. There has to be no self-deception in this.

The rule of chastity needs to be understood in the same sense. It signifies mainly that we must be in control of our desires, our lower sensuality and our sexual imagination. It would be a mistake to try and achieve this aim by forcible suppression of natural processes. If we perform the prescribed exercises and give our sensual impulses a different concentration point from the usual, these natural processes will be cleansed, and raised to a higher plane of experience. We shall no longer be lost in these things. Chastity in thought, word and deed is our goal. If we concentrate our energies and wishes on the goal, we shall begin to get results. Higher powers and abilities will be developed by the very act of striving for it. Even if we fall short, we shall discover that the important thing is to make a consistent effort to reach this goal.

Students are faced with another inescapable command: all life must be respected and spared. Even if we come across what appears to be a loathsome creature, we ought to consider that its life is part of the One Life and that it has a spiritual aspect. The eternal moves in it. I am not sitting in judgment on those who do not obey this command. But for those who have decided to tread the path, it is unavoidable.

Because yoga strives to come to the truth, it is obvious that students must develop truthfulness. How could it be otherwise? The quality of truth that can be attained is very high. It is spiritual truth in its own spiritual domain. Truth is capable of being experienced in *manas*, the "I am." Christ's words, "I am the truth," gives us some inkling of the spiritual experience that arises out of the communion of the higher self with cosmic verity. Truth can be known in the "I am" and can be assimilated with ourselves.[6]

Second Stage (Niyama)

The second stage on the path requires of us further self-discipline with a view to inner and outer purity. External rules of cleanliness, such as our Western hygiene, do not lead to the true goal. Inner and outer have to be equally clean, and we

---

[6] "I am the truth" here is an abridged version of Christ's words in John 14:6. Actually, He is not talking about an experience of identification with the truth, but is offering Himself to His disciples as the truth itself. *Tr.*

need to strive for purity in the functions of thinking, feeling and willing. Nothing less than purity is consistent with the truth.

To describe this, I am reminded of the scene in the Gospel where Jesus washed His disciples' feet. With their feet human beings move to the performance of deeds, and deeds become destiny. In deed and destiny works the will of mankind. So foot-washing signifies that the human will must be cleansed from the ground up, from its very foundations. This would apply especially to the disciples, who had committed themselves to following in their Master's footsteps. The outer ritual symbolized an internal spiritual process. Things enacted on the lowest plane, that of the senses, can happen invisibly at the same time on the spiritual plane, and then have a meaning that is quite different. From this example we can see the difference between truth in the spiritual and truth in the physical world.[7]

Will-power must also be cleansed if we mean to get closer to the goal striven for in yoga, and we have to walk, so to speak, to the position where we can act and influence our destiny. Yet, in the second stage on the yoga path, the aim is to cultivate contentment. This is done by becoming reconciled to our fate. Every struggle against the latter blocks the road to freedom.

There should be no question of trying to repress every feeling of dissatisfaction with our lot. That would eventually sow the seeds of illnesses, and illnesses are not the aim of yoga. We need to be reconciled to our fate, and this can happen only when we recognize that higher laws are at work in our lives, and that these laws are administered by the higher self. If we

---

[7] The footwashing was contrasted with the bath and meant the removal of daily defilement picked up after a general spiritual cleansing. It was also performed as a lesson in humility, none of the disciples having volunteered to accept the menial task (see John 13). The author's exegesis takes a different line from this. *Tr.*

heed and accept the laws of reincarnation and karma (rebirth and self-created fate); then the world will look different.

Fate is not an alien visitation, it is not something weird—we made it ourselves—in former life, and in accordance with causal law. Where fate is concerned, people act as if they were in a trance-induced state, at every moment allowing themselves to be carried along by what is happening around them. This, we say, has nothing to do with us, it is fate; but it has to do with us, it is the harvest of the past. And yet we can be free—free now to decide our future fate by looking to our behavior before the Wheel of the Law of cause and effect begins to turn for us again. But we are not free from the past.

In no way does this concept contradict the teachings of Christianity. Christ taught His disciples that nobody shall come out from thence (prison) till he has paid the uttermost farthing. (Matthew 5:26). Now this is the law of karma![8] We are subject to it.

The purification and refining of our souls in connection with the raising of our thought processes to our own inner light makes possible a degree of consciousness in which we can create our fate and our future. And so, freedom and necessity are both bound up in our fate. The higher knowledge of the law of karma makes it possible for us to achieve a state of spiritual balance. Our higher ego is the spiritual hypomochlion (fulcrum) of the scales of our fate and of our mental life. Through the study prescribed for the stage known as Niyama, we can attain the inner peace that balances the scales in which our moods swing up and down. Through insight we acquire

---

[8] The passage to which the author refers reads: "Agree with thine adversary quickly, whiles thou art in the way with him; lest at any time the adversary deliver thee to the judge; and the judge deliver thee to the officer, and thou be cast into prison. Verily I say unto thee, Thou shalt by no means come out thence, till thou hast paid the uttermost farthing (last dime)"; Evidentally, "out-of-court" settlements are best in religion too! *Tr.*

poise, knowing that whatever must happen will happen. We need to wait patiently for our hour to come. We need to learn to face the world with assured calm. In Matthew (chapter 5) we read, "Blessed are the peacemakers: for they shall be called the children of God." "Children of God" means those who manage to let their higher nature express itself.

Before starting practice, the yoga student was required to open up spiritually, mentally, and physically to a nobler concept of life. The student had to be genuinely seeking spiritual truth, and was asked to turn from the things that bind the soul to the earthly, so he or she could concentrate on a loftier goal. For this, a process of purification was required. Holy texts were studied until their meaning became clear. For us, too, these texts reveal how spiritual laws affect the fate of each individual. They extend our view beyond the brief span of life and death, to take in our prenatal and post-mortem existence in the spheres.

A true knowledge of these relationships helps us face our destiny with equanimity. Only when we possess the inner peace of mind that demands nothing of fate have we progressed sufficiently to start the onerous exercises. Our fate will be in accordance with our striving, if we are mature enough. But I must point out that there is no such thing as a permanent state of mental calm. It is essential to cultivate the ability to restore our equilibrium at all times.

A word is in order here on the study of "holy texts." The writer of the foreword, Dr. H. H. von Veltheim, says in his unpublished *Aphorisms* that "to read and understand so-called sacred books and the majority of Eastern esoteric writing, we modern Americans and Europeans need something that is not yet available, a dictionary compiled by a Western esotericist." Today we no longer have direct access to the old scripts because our consciousness has shifted. A key is needed to unlock them, but finding it is no easy task.

Third Stage (Asana)

Not until we reach Asana, the third stage of the study of Yoga, do we receive instructions on posture (Asanas). Now, where posture is concerned, allowance must be made for the fact that we are no longer as supple as people were in the days of Patanjali—although Orientals have been more successful than we have been in preserving flexibility. The celebrated old sitting postures of yoga are no longer essential. If they were, contortionists would make the best yogis.

It is obvious that the aphorisms concerning the third stage relate to the physical body and to the limbs in particular. The Asanas associated with them were a product of their time, suited to the Eastern people for whom they were prescribed. However, the occidental constitution is not exactly the same as the oriental. In the sitting posture shown in Figure 1 (on page 20) the special placement of the feet causes the internal life forces to circulate in a closed lemniscate (a figure eight), with the result that the yogin can rest completely in himself or herself, *outside* the macrocosm, so to speak. In our own age, we are familiar with the idea of space travel, and we are coming to see ourselves as spiritual beings *inside* a cosmic world. Therefore we need a meditation Asana that is different from the traditional ones.

The main requirement of meditation is stability. We need to relax in one place. We should not try to meditate lying down—that is to say, in a horizontal position. We are distinguished from animals by our upright stance; so, if we desire to reach higher states of consciousness, we must remain vertical. A horizontal position would lead to states of reduced awareness (dreams, sleep, deep sleep). We do not need to stand when meditating, we can sit. Both feet should be on the floor, the eyes should be open and looking straight ahead. Initially, the hands can be clasped. The hands will automatically separate

Figure 1. The centers or Lotuses.

after meditation has begun. A convenient resting place for them is on the thighs near the knees, where they should lie lightly in the extended position. The posture must be steady and relaxed, with no tension anywhere. Once we feel comfortable, the body can become the instrument of the spirit.

Fourth Stage (Pranayama)

The fourth stage, as the name Pranayama implies, has to do with controlling the breath. Life and breath are inseparable. We live in an ocean of air, containing light and heat that enter us with our breathing. The fourth stage is not concerned with the physical structures of the body, but with its animating principle. Respiration is rhythmic, and has a one to four relationship with the heartbeat. The action of the heart and lungs maintains the rhythms of air-flow and liquid-flow in us.

Life in our earthly existence depends on breathing and on the circulation of blood. The normal healthy adult breathes 18 times per minute and has a pulse rate of ca. 72 beats per minute. As I have just said, the two cycles are in the ratio of one to four. These rhythms connect human beings directly to the cosmos. In the approximately 18-year Saros period (of eclipses), the Moon has a rhythm that is a quarter of that of the spring Sun. The latter takes 72 years to move backward through one zodiac degree (precession of the equinoxes). Again, 72 years is the average measure of human life. And the 18-year cycle can be recognized in human life also—the fire of life blazes up again. I refer to these connections simply in passing, and then only to show the relationship between cosmic rhythms and the rhythm of life.

There is a natural link between the rhythmic breathing of air and light and the rhythmic pumping of blood and lymph round the body. They go together, as well as having their parallels in the macrocosmic world (since we are born from the cosmos). If we draw about 18 breaths per minute while the pulse rate is 72 beats per minute, we shall be in harmony inwardly with the currents of the macrocosm and, in particular, with those of the Moon and Sun. We may discover that this harmony puts us in tune with the world process, yet also note with surprise that it lowers rather than raises consciousness. Heraclitus uttered the dark saying, "War is the father of all." This is as much as to say that it is the *opposing* forces of the universe that constitute and make it possible. Unremitting harmony can lull us into peaceful slumber while strife sharpens our awareness. We need to keep this in mind.

So students who individualize and control their respiration will be able to influence the life processes flowing through the physical body. Little by little the inner currents will be mastered and imbued with consciousness. Each chakra or lotus will then be able to unfold at the places where yogic doctrine shows them to exist. Just as the Demiurge was the Spirit behind all that is becoming and has become, so the human spirit can intentionally bring about the production of hormones and vitamins and other body activators and can distribute them and direct them in the organism; all this by means of the linkage between the life currents, chakras and glands. There are discoveries waiting to be made about the human body that are more significant than the results of atom smashing. All we can do here is to allude to these possibilities. For my own part, I hope that our contemporaries will not be able to find out these secrets of life—their morals do not seem to advance with their technology. And when morals and technology are out of step, a knowledge of the things we have discovered could lead to new human catastrophe.

In the fourth stage on the path, we are concerned with breath control that alters the state of the body to one of repose. At this point, I should like to quote one of the unpublished *Aphorisms* of Dr. von Veltheim. He writes, "When the Indian holy man, my guru, Sri Ramana Maharshi, was asked about the nature and value of breathing practices (Pranayama), he replied: It is easier to govern the courage than the breath. The former is like trying to milk a cow by force, the latter is like coming with a bunch of grass and stroking her on the back." In the fourth stage we are still in the outer court of the sanctuary, which is entered only in meditation. Ramana Maharshi perceived today's breathing practices more as a kind of technique. But this does not mean that the same was true 2000 years ago. At that time, the breath and its regulation had a greater significance than it does today, especially in ancient India. Anyway, it must be realized that the technical control of the breath is quite useless if the other conditions of yogic study are not fulfilled.

Just as the whole point of adopting a certain posture of the body is to prevent the arms and legs from getting in the way, to enable them to become an instrument of the spirit, so the living rhythms are turned into instruments of the spirit through which the bodily condition can be brought into a state of complete rest. The breathing process can be individualized; that is to say it can be removed from unison with the Cosmic. Exhalation can be deliberately prolonged to twice the time taken for inhalation. After exhalation, the breath is then held for three times as long as the inhalation. Exhalation should be complete and the navel should be drawn in at the end of it.

As we breathe in, we should imagine the mysteries of the universe entering our bodies. On the other hand, when we breathe out, we should imagine our own being uniting with the universe. This must be done consciously. For that reason, a pause is made not after inhalation but after exhalation. Nowadays, human beings are starting to impress their spirit on the cosmos that once refashioned them. We were once formed from the cosmos; then we would retain what we had breathed in from outside.

Today the opposite holds true "All things are flowing," asserted Heraclitus. Everything changes, everything undergoes metamorphosis. Therefore we must not cling dogmatically to principles meant to help people from 2000 years ago; our distance from them in time and space necessitates certain modifications. Students have to achieve an elastic, individual, conscious mode of respiration during practice today. This is possible when the technique is no longer forced but automatic, and the attention can turn freely to the higher stages of meditation.

Fifth Stage (Pratyahara)

The fifth stage is the conscious mastery of the senses. To recapitulate: after complete repose of the body (generally stage three), came control of the body rhythms in preparation for the spiritual concentration necessary to stage four. Now, in stage five, the objective is to rule the senses and ideation. Therefore what we are dealing with here is the sensory nervous system, which is concentrated chiefly in the head.

We must try to bring tranquillity to the whole physical organization from bottom to top. Only after "stilling the storm" that rages in human beings is it possible to release those forces that are able to penetrate to the supersensual regions. Spiritual forces are continually active in the body's organization, but we remain unaware of them. When they are brought to rest as described, they can be used in different ways. We can then experience ourselves as spiritual egos, as manas.

In the normal human ego is found everything that is experienced through the connection between soul and body. A higher stage than this, which can be reached in meditation even when fully conscious, when soul and body have fallen silent, is experiencing and coming to know the perennial "I" that comes from the realm of pure spirit beings. The lowest level of the higher, purely spiritual, enduring self is called *Manas*. In order to perceive the spiritual, we need to train our spiritual organs of perception. We possess these in embryo, but they have to be consciously developed.

Before these spiritual organs can be developed and used, we have to become absolute rulers of our sense impressions and ideas. The main battle involves the senses, and is fought on the field of perception. This mastery is essential, because consciousness awakens at the gates of the senses. Students must practice closing these gates and yet staying alert.

In no way must the closing of the senses be construed as falling asleep. In meditation, consciousness is heightened, not lowered. However, we could say that the events of sleep are experienced in the waking state, and that meditators learn about the other side of life, the one we usually sleep through.

What method, then, must we use to rule our sense impressions, our external perceptions, and also their echoes in memory? The answer lies in patient, repetitious practice employing one-pointed thought and feeling. Behind each object stands something that is immaterial; the external shape and colors only reveal part of it, while the other, unseen, part is spiritual. By intense physical perception (e.g. by crystal gazing), it is possible to achieve a simple type of meditation. After a time that varies with the individual, the object will present itself vividly in the mind, at which point specific inner effects will be perceived. Then, if we are sufficiently advanced, we shall be so rapt that all external sense impressions will disappear. Our inner senses will awaken and we shall perceive the interior of the object under examination.

I do not mean that the inner material substance will be seen; no, what will be observed is the spiritual will underlying what has become a material object. The object's true nature is revealed as the veil of Maya becomes transparent. Maya, or illusion, persists until we stop thinking that visible forms and colors are all there is to know about objects.

Meditation is an activity through which our being expands, and objects we have always regarded as external seem to be internal. They are experienced as "really real." First comes the feeling that the self has undergone cosmic expansion. As the physical senses close, so the supersensual faculties open—provided the meditation is strong and vivid.

This stage includes phases of meditation that proceed from mineral through vegetable through animal through human. Interested Western readers can find further information on the subject in *Knowledge of the Higher Worlds And its Attainment* a book by Rudolf Steiner.[9] In the meditation process, there are many opportunities to go wrong. Indiscriminate meditation should be avoided, and we should keep to the forms that have been tried and tested over the centuries by various spiritual teachers. Those who want to go the way that leads to being able to practice Pranayama in an atmosphere of spiritual light are recommended to make a careful study of the above-mentioned book, which was written to help people avoid circuitous and misleading routes. Except where they are needed to clarify what happens in yoga, further details of meditation practice will be omitted here, as they do not serve our present purpose.

Sense impressions impinge from outside; ideas come from inside. Their actions are diametrically opposed. By proper use of imagination, we can pierce the veil of sense impressions to discover the moving spirit behind the object. This takes us to a higher level, but this will also bring a change of direction—a retrogression of the sensory process to its *status nascendi* (nascent state). We become one with the object of our contemplation, so to speak, so that it expresses its true nature in our soul. This, though perhaps sounding strange, is open to verification. There is nothing in yoga that can not be experienced if the conditions are right.

So far, all our work has been preparatory. The inevitability of the logic behind it springs from the fact that the higher man or woman is at work on the lower. We are attempting to free

---

[9] Rudolf Steiner, *Knowledge of the Higher Worlds and its Attainment* (Hudson, NY: Anthroposophic Press, 1947).

the mental processes from the body. Our first move is to address ourselves to the moral problems of the will-sphere, where we need to be cleansed from the stains picked up by the once pure soul through its involvement with the earth-world. Normally, the will pushes outward with demands and deeds but, as it cooperates with our moral side, it starts moving the other way. Thus the aim of the preliminary practice is to bring about a reversal of the direction of the will, which then no longer flows out to the world, but toward the inner being's moral center of gravity. Obviously a change of will of this sort bestows higher powers. Moral substance, and with it the essential nature of the individual are changed. It is important that we do not neglect outer world obligations, which need to be rigorously fulfilled. The change is only an inner one.

Next comes the change in the intensity of the rhythmic processes of human life. When these are controlled by the spirit, a change in feelings can take place. Feelings are especially concentrated in the chest, where the respiratory and circulatory processes have their organs—the lungs and heart.

Finally, we consider the conversion of the life of the mind into something supersensual. The mind is concentrated in the head. The higher mind needs to be extricated from its involvement with the lower mind and its involvement with matter. The intention is to release the functions of willing, feeling and thinking from the physical body. To the extent that we succeed, there is an opening up of the organs of supersensual perception. The latter are the chakras, which we shall be dealing with in the following chapters.

The will is directed inward to the depths of the personal being and primeval law (analogous to "Father"). The feelings are intensified, and spread out horizontally to include a universal sympathy for all creatures, so that a great love is felt embracing the cosmos (analogous to "Son"). The thoughts are sent upward to the free heights of the universal divine Spirit (analagous to "Spirit" or, as some would say, to the "Heavenly Virgin").

Sixth Stage (Dharana)

According to the *Yoga Sutra*, the next three stages of training introduce us to meditation proper. The sixth stage begins with concentration (*Dharana*), in which the attention is fixed on a point. However, success will elude us here unless we have mastered the earlier stages to the extent that we will not be disturbed by the physical body with its life forces, sensations and appetites. The soul must be like a calm lake. So concentration is preceded by composure. Once this has been attained, the practice starts in which thinking is released from the ties that bind it to its organ, the physical brain.

To begin with, thought content has something concrete about it. We contemplate an image, but one that has a symbolic character. As we concentrate more strongly on the spiritual purport of the symbol, the image recedes little by little into the background. The ordinary world of the senses disappears as the activity of the soul becomes detached from it. Life now begins in the realm of Ideas. First of all, meditators have the impression that they are doing the thinking: "I think." But, once the image being contemplated has vanished, the thought-world itself is perceived. Then meditators find universal thinking processes going on inside. "I think" is replaced by the clear realization that "thinking is going on in me." The "thinker" seems to have no part to play in the thinking processes.

After the life is withdrawn from the external sense organs (at stage 5), it goes on to withdraw from the physical organ of thought, the mind, in stage 6. Then thinking becomes completely abstract and has no more life in it; it is carried on seemingly by the "death process." The abstract thought is pure thought, bare thought without life. And so, at stage six, the lowest peak of the spiritual world is scaled. The "I am" is experienced through *Manas*. It is "Manna" or heavenly food.[10]

Seventh Stage (Dhyana)

This stage is, at the same time, stage two of the three-part process of meditation, and is called *Dhyana*, or contemplation. In general, Dhyana is taken to mean meditation, although it is only the kingpin, not the whole, of this. Strength has to be developed to remain in this condition at this stage. Yogins only have this strength if they have previously really expanded their feelings to the world horizon, so that their active intensified love has become universal. For what returns in a spiritual form at stage seven, and has the appearance of a transcendental power, is emotion altered by the spirit. The spiritualized action of the heart and lungs (the aim of stage four) now joins forces with the abstract, but still dead, mental imagery of stage six. The simple product of the imagination is imbued with spiritual strength and life. It is as if something spiritual has been hatched. If stage six sees the successful unfolding into experience of the Manas, so the seventh stage leads to *Buddhi* (understanding), where contact with life is renewed—the wine of life is added to the bread.

---

[10] This is just an analogy of course. *Manas* and *Manna* sound the same, but that is as far as it goes. *Manas* is Indian and is defined by Rama Prasad in *Nature's Finer Forces* (Madras, India: Theosophical Publishing House, 1947) as: "Mind; the third principle of the universe from below." *Manna*, on the other hand, is Hebrew. Professor W. L. Roy, in his *A Complete Hebrew and English Critical and Pronouncing Dictionary* (New York, 1837) says that the word is "derived from *Manna*, a part, portion as of food and *hoo*, him, i.e., God. The bread of God, or of eternal life. Ex. 16:31. See John 6:58." *Tr.*

Eighth Stage (Samadhi)

The eighth stage is that of *Samadhi*, or submersion in deepest devotion. The meditator rests immobile in respect of thinking, feeling, willing, and the processes of the physical shell. The communion of the human spirit with the divine spirit of truth affects matter itself. It is possible to reach beyond Manas and Buddhi to the highest part of our nature that is open to experience during our sojourn on earth, namely *Atman* (the individual soul or life-force), the seed of which is buried in each physical human being. What comes in, in a new way, on top of the transformed thoughts and emotions, is the transformed will. This subdues matter, and can eventually dissolve it in that spiritual will, that creative energy that first set the world on its way. Here we are face to face with the supreme wonder of the transmutation of substance through the incorporation of spirituality with human will, which can be reconsecrated. Samadhi occurs in utter stillness, yet with the highest activity of the will. It is the loftiest stage known to the yoga system.

For thousands of years, the Hindu cast of mind has favored tolerance. There is no insistence that the path of the human spirit to communion with the universal spirit has to follow a rigid route.[11] Indeed, it would be foolish to be doctrinaire. It is certain, however, that union with the self-subsisting universal

---

[11] There are numerous yoga paths, but they are not mutually exclusive. It is their approaches that differ. Hatha Yoga emphasizes the physical body, Gnani Yoga concentrates on the formation of pure knowledge, Bhakti Yoga is concerned with transcendent love and devotion to God, Raja Yoga (the royal way of raja) has to do with the highest stages of meditation. From a higher point of view, one can say that the individual systems have an inner relationship like, for example, the four Evangelists of the New Testament and the four Signs of the Sphinx: Bull-Lion-Eagle-Water Carrier (Human). The subject stands in need of synthesizing. Kundalini Yoga, which many exponents say is the highest form of yoga, aims at the union of what is "eternal" in male and female. The eternal feminine attains union with the eternal masculine in the Thousand-petaled Lotus.

truth, its power and substance, is possible only through the freeing of the psychic functions from their physical organs. These functions have to be enhanced and lifted. Buddhist teachings draw essentially sharper distinctions between the individual stages of meditation. Professor Hermann Beckh gives some valuable information about this in his *Buddhismus*.[12] Personally, I find the difference between the three stages comprising meditation proper in the system set out in the Yoga Sutras to be especially clear; the reason being that they result in the transformation of ordinary willing, feeling and thinking by the concentrated human spirit. What is more, they are related to the three transcendental sheaths of the higher human ego, known in India as the Manasic, Buddhic and Atmic.

The Samadhi condition of contemplation is still reached, even today, by only a few great souls in India, and will not be easily attained by Westerners either.

---

[12] H. Beckh, *Buddhismus,* 1928.

PART TWO

THE ROOTS OF POWER

The Location of the Chakras
in the Human Body

For the exterior description of the chakras (Cakras) that follows, I am relying on two works on Tantric Yoga.[1] These are the 55-verse *Satcakra Nirupana* which deals with six chakras and the Sahasrara, and *Paduka-Pancaka*, the five-legged footstool, which in seven verses celebrates the Thousand-petaled Lotus.

Arthur Avalon translated the verses and the learned Hindu commentary in his *The Serpent Power*.[2] The account of the six centers and the commentary form part of the Sritattva-cintamani of Sri Purnandayati. The illustrations in his book are also presented here. The lotus petals, their shapes, colors, sounds, special contents, tattwas, and so forth belong to a tradition thousands of years old. Originally, these details were perceived by seers. Avalon's work has been adopted as my starting point.

Avalon's book has a purely scientific value. In what follows, on the other hand, my emphasis will be on the spiritual aspects of the chakras, which we must learn to recognize if we

---

[1] The literal meaning of Tantra is weaving. The subject is expounded in many esoteric books of a special magical-mystical and magical-sacred character.

[2] Arthur Avalon, *The Serpent Power* (New York: Dover, 1974; Madras, India: Ganesh & Co., 1918).

plan to set out on the path leading to transcendental knowledge. In spite of many years' study, the obvious connections did not become clear to me until I had studied the extremely valuable works of Dr. Rudolf Steiner.

Figure 1 on page 20 shows the connection between the individual chakras and the spine. This connection is regarded in some systems as very close, in others as fairly loose. The little circles in the sketch represent manifestations of life-energy seen by clairvoyants and are known as lotuses or chakras (i.e., wheels or cakras). In those who have reached a certain degree of development, the chakras start to rotate; whereas in those who have not undergone this development, the petals droop inactively and look dark and colorless. The term wheel comes from this turning motion, and the description of the chakras as blossoms is metaphorical, too. According to the number of petals, we speak of the two-, four-, twelve-petaled Lotus, etc. When consciousness has been placed in the centers the petals begin to spread. A teacher is able to tell from the colors of the petals how far the students have progressed and what they may be doing wrong. The spinal column is called the inner *Meru* (a mythical Indian mountain on which the heavenly ocean once fell). Symbolically, the human head is like the roof of the world, an inner Himalaya. It takes great effort to climb the mountain; and, in the same way, great effort is required to reach the top of our inner Himalaya through the centers. Two ducts for the life currents wind left and right about the central column, or spinal cord, as may be seen in figure 1.

> On the left is the feminine Ida, associated with the Moon; on the right is the masculine Pingala, associated with the Sun; in the middle is Sushumna, the substance of the threefold quality (the Gunas)."[3]

---

[3] From Verse 1, "Sat-Cakra-Nirupana," in *The Serpent Power* by Arthur Avalon (New York: Dover, 1974; Madras, India: Ganesh & Co., 1918), p. 320.

Neither ida nor pingala keep to one side of the spine, but weave from side to side, crossing it three times in all. Because they also meet at the beginning and end of their course, they touch five times. The pattern they make is similar to that of the caduceus (Mercury's staff). Corresponding to where the latter ends in a golden apple, there is the subsidiary Three-petaled nasal Lotus—the point where the three great streams meet (the 7th chakra). This is quite close to the better-known Two-petaled Lotus between the eyebrows (or 6th chakra).

The stimulating masculine current (pingala), which starts on the right, is dark red, like blood issuing from the heart; the calming feminine current (ida), which starts on the left, is pale pink, like the blood of the lungs. Respiration oxygenates the blood that comes to the lungs from the heart, and turns it bright red. However, the feminine current is often shown as blue, like venous blood after oxygen has been given up to the cells in return for carbonic acid. There is no contradiction between yoga and physiology here; yoga is simply looking at the process further down the line. The Sun and Moon to which the verse refers are not, of course, the astronomical Sun and Moon, but spiritual principles. The two currents correspond to the building-up and breaking-down forces in nature. The yogin learns to combine them in a single balanced force.

As a lunar current, ida has an affinity with the high potencies of silver. Pingala, on the other hand, has an affinity with those of gold, and sushumna with those of lead.

Just as the spine is compared with Mount Meru, so ida is compared by the Hindus with Ganga (the Ganges), pingala with Yamuna (the Jumna) and sushumna with Sarasvati, the three great rivers of India.[4] "As above, so below" is an old esoteric dictum, and the truth of it is seen in the relationship

---

[4] There are other great and historic rivers, such as the Indus and the Brahmaputra, but the three mentioned flow together like the channels in the spine. What is more, they flow through the old "Middle Kingdom" of the Brahmans. *Tr.*

of our planet earth and of the whole cosmos to the human being. "*Tat tvam asi*," "Thou art That" says the guru (teacher) to the chela (student), and points to the outside world. Everything in the universe has a real equivalent in the interior of the body. The individual is the cosmos on a small scale; the cosmos is the individual on a large scale—a sidereal scale in fact.

The two lateral currents are also inside the spine in Sushumna. The awakened force can ascend straight up the center of the spine as if these two lateral currents and sushumna were one. The central current is itself threefold. Sushumna contains the finer Vajrini channel and also the Chitrini.[5] Verse 2[6] tells us that "their substance is composed of pure intelligence." But Avalon interprets the two currents as ganglia that are very closely linked with the solar plexus. Beckh, on the other hand, treats them as occult arteries. Actually, it is a mistake to think of them in purely physical, material terms. The Ida, Pingala and Sushumna are by no means the same thing as the anatomical spine. We need to understand that the physical organs are no more than the material counterparts of a system of forces— a system of formative forces that acts as the architect of the organs, etc. At the basis of the familiar spinal cord is another, elementary, one that is not open to ordinary perception. To people in possession of spiritual knowledge, it is clear that everything human has its positive pole in the living force field and its negative pole in the material world. If we talk of nothing but ganglia, we are limiting our view to the negative result of a supersensual activity. A sensation only needs the nerve currents in order to be felt by the physical body. From the caused we ought to turn to the cause, from the dead (matter is dead) to the living. The currents known as *Nadis* are "tubules," for that is what the word means. However, they are present only in the living body, in the system of living formative forces that

---

[5] Vajrini being symbolized as gray matter and Chitrini, the central canal.

[6] Verse 2 of the "Sat-Cakra-Nirupana," as translated by Arthur Avalon in *The Serpent Power.*

interpenetrate the physical body until death; 72,000 nadis in all are said to carry the flow of life forces.

The lower five chakras can be roughly described in terms of their position relative to the spine. This is anatomically divided into five regions.

1) The coccygeal region—five incompletely formed vertebrae, the last two of which are usually completely fused together, form the coccyx. The Four-petaled Lotus belongs here (1st chakra).

2) The sacral region—consisting of five vertebrae united by the sacrum. The Six-petaled Lotus belongs here (2nd chakra).

3) The lumbar region—consisting of five vertebrae. The Ten-petaled navel Lotus belongs here (3rd chakra).

4) The shoulder region—consisting of twelve vertebrae. The Twelve-petaled heart Lotus belongs here (4th chakra).

5) The neck region—consisting of seven vertebrae. The Sixteen-petaled throat Lotus belongs here (5th chakra).

According to the Nirupana, different substances progressively graded from coarse to fine belong to the centers as shown in Table 1. In these substances six different *Devis* (goddesses, whom we can regard as impetus-giving and causative natural forces) hold sway:

Table 1. Goddess substance and chakra relationships.

Devi	Substance	Lotus
Shākini	Bone substance	4-petaled
Kākini	Fat substance	6-petaled
Lākini	Flesh substance	10-petaled
Rākini	Blood substance	12-petaled
Dākini	Skin substance	16-petaled
Hākini	Marrow substance	2-petaled

The way the centers are arranged allows us to group them quite easily within three regions. Thus the Four-petaled and Six-petaled Lotuses (1st and 2nd chakras) come within the Fire Region (Agni), i.e., within the region of metabolism with its digestive processes, and of sex with its appetites. This is the region of the will, which is still obscure to modern men and women. The divine powers of nature rule in it still. The Hindus say that these two centers belong to the Guna known as *Tamas*. The Gunas are qualities of the psychic life, and comprise *Tamas* (apathy), *Rajas* (passion), which promotes development, and *Sattwa* (wisdom).

To the Rajas, or middle region, belong the Ten-petaled and Twelve-petaled Lotuses (navel and heart chakras). Respiration takes place in the chest as far down as the diaphragm. The emotions are very closely bound up with the heart. In the heart we experience things in a half-awake, dreamy sort of way.

The Sixteen-petaled and Two-petaled Lotuses belong to the Sattwa region (the lotuses of the throat and forehead chakras). Here is the seat of language, thought and understanding. Here people are most fully conscious or awake.

These three regions have been assigned to the personified planets, (Saturnian) fire (Agni), the sun (Surya), and the moon (Chandra). They also represent three stages of consciousness (sleeping, dreaming, waking), the three psychic functions of willing, feeling and thinking, and the physical activities of metabolism, of respiration and circulation, and of communication via the nerves. One passage tells of the process:

> Now I speak of the first sprouting shoot
> (of the Yoga plant)
> of complete realization of the Brahman,
> which is to be achieved,
> according to the Tantras,

by means of the six Cakras and so forth
in their proper order.[7]

The Indian divine triad finds its counterpart in the three regions
of the body. In the lowermost part Rudra-Shiva (the red Shiva)
rules. Shiva is a god with many names and as many aspects. He
himself has a threefold nature, for he is creator and destroyer
in one and, in the middle position of balance, preserver as well.
Shiva is Pashupati, i.e., lord of all creatures. Pashu means
creature. He is active in the region of metabolism and of the
reproductive drive, and thus at the physically creative pole of
the individual. Rudra-Shiva is "lord of the physical," also the
destroyer of disease. This implies the use of the catabolic and
anabolic processes found in Ida and Pingala.

The physical creative pole, based in the metabolic system,
is counterbalanced by the spiritual creative pole in the head.
The polarity of light and darkness corresponds to that of mind
and sex (or metabolism), or of thinking and willing. Darkness
is associated with matter, the inner light with spirit. The lower
pole of the cold luminous flame is heavy, the upper pole has
little weight. Thus Shiva, as part of a Trinity, may be thought
of as a "Father," whose primeval law embodies nature, humanity and all created things. He is the invisible creative and de-
vouring fire that resides in our physical creative pole. Brahma
resembles the Spirit of the Christian scheme. Vishnu, the preserver, occupies the middle region, that of the heart. His godhead is "Son-like."

A similar trinity is that of Isis, Horus, and Osiris of the
Egyptians. The three body-regions mentioned above also correspond to the Manvantaras, great eras through which our
world has already passed. The world was created by the will of
God. From Him it grew to life. In the third metamorphosis of

---

[7] *The Serpent Power*, "Sat-Cakra-Nirupana," p. 317.

the world, the life became the light of humanity. Living, as we do, in today's fourth state of the world, we carry the three developmental stages within us. But, in the three regions, lie the seeds of higher worlds and of higher states of consciousness.

> *In the head is the predisposition to Manas,*
> *In the heart to Buddhi,*
> *In the digestive organs to Atma.*

The Yogin encounters these seeds in concentration and meditation. He or she nurtures and germinates them. In the lowest lives the highest. "The last shall be first."

The development of our higher potential signifies the reparation of the so-called "Fall," the release from death and matter, as well as our adoption into child status by God—something that Paul tells us is eagerly awaited by all creatures.

Cosmic Aspects

If we connect the chakra centers in such a way that the resulting curve is a spiral winding round the spine to left and right, we get the shape of the caduceus. Our solar system turns in space in spiral-form on the way to the apex in Hercules. The same law governs humanity as governs the universe.

The backbone can be seen as a sort of inner ecliptic—a lunar ecliptic in which the 30 vertebrae correspond to the 30 days of the moon. The consciousness that moves through this center is like the sun. The solstices of the inner sun are in the head (winter) and in the genitals (summer).

Goethe regarded the head as an expanded, tilted vertebra. The Two-petaled and Thousand-petaled Lotuses lie in the head. To that extent they are free from the spine, whereas the other Lotuses are fettered to it. If Goethe was right, the two cranial Lotuses would be connected with a metamorphosed vertebra, and would be at liberty to develop a free consciousness of a different nature from the more primitive, dull, animal-like consciousness of a spine built along the horizontal plane. Corresponding to the planetary spheres we have:

The 4-petaled Lotus of the interior human
    Moon sphere,
The 6-petaled Lotus of the interior human
    Mercury sphere,
The 10-petaled Lotus of the interior human
    Venus sphere,
The 12-petaled Lotus of the interior human
    Sun sphere,
The 16-petaled Lotus of the interior human
    Mars sphere,
The 2-petaled Lotus of the interior human
    Jupiter sphere,
The 1000-petaled Lotus of the interior human
    Saturn sphere.

In *Eine kurtze Eröfnung und Anweisung der dreyen Prinzipien und Welten im Menschen* ("A Brief Communication and Advice Concerning the Three Principles and Worlds in Man"), published in 1696 by Johan Georg Graber and Johan Georg Gichtel, the above-mentioned places assigned to the chakras are marked with planets. Nothing is said in their little book about the chakras of course, but it is obvious that an identity exists between the "planets in the body" and the chakras.[8]

The spheres also correspond to "world months," or cycles of development. In our ascent from a condition typified by the moon, or the Four-petaled Lotus, we have now reached—and are still occupying after 2000 years!—the sphere of Jupiter, the sphere of the Two-petaled Lotus in the forehead between the eyebrows. Each era has its own Lotus-state of development as

---

[8] Gichtel was a disciple of the famous German mystic Boehme, who wrote two books on the "Three Principles." *Tr.*

LIVERPOOL
JOHN MOORES UNIVERSITY
AVRIL ROBARTS LRC
TEL. 0151 231 4022

Table 2. Stages of development.

Historical Era	Lotus-state of Development	Time Perspective
Very ancient India	4-petaled Lotus	
Very ancient Persian	6-petaled Lotus	
Egyptian-Babylonian-Chaldean	10-petaled Lotus	Past
Egyptian period of Akhenaten	12-petaled Lotus	
Greco-Roman	16-petaled Lotus	
Central European	2-petaled Lotus	Present
Modern World	1000-petaled Lotus	Future

shown in Table 2. Thus the "yoga plant" grows in the human soul and determines the character of various cultures.

It would take us too far afield, if I were to discuss the links between cultural change and changes of disposition. But there is no doubt that in the old pre-Christian cultures the life of the organs was much more vivid than it is today. This life-sense gave perceptions of internal organs, indeed of the organism as a whole, and bestowed a keener realization of raised or lowered vitality and of such things as hunger and thirst, than we possess now. The old clairvoyance was largely governed by the organs. This ability and others are nowadays more submerged in the subconscious, as evidenced by deep (mesoblastic) sensibility. It is the sense of sight that we rely on most. We form our concepts by means of observation and thought. The change is analogous to what happens when the focus of attention changes from one chakra to another. As I have already said, it is impossible to go into the subject in detail here; however, it is hoped that enough has been said to show how the Two-petaled Lotus belongs especially to our present culture and why it has to be developed.

Kundalini

What is kundalini? She is the highest Shakti, the first and highest birth-giving, cosmic power. In her main aspect she is Aditi, mother of the Adityas. Her names are various. She is Ishvari, the "all-powerful virgin" and also the serpent. The serpent should be regarded as the old clairvoyant consciousness. This was tied up with the organs and the spine. The old knowledge rested on clairmindedness. Intellectual activity was not yet abstract, not emancipated from the feelings to the degree it is today.

Years ago the center of gravity of thought was displaced from the middle region of the body to the site that essentially belongs to the spinal column, namely the nervous system of the head. The ancient wisdom was able to perceive the process in the image of the lifting up of the serpent. The spine has a serpentine form. Those who understand how to insinuate their being into the spine have to be snake-like.

Kundalini is Mātrika, the genetrix of the whole universe. Since she is mother of all, she is no one's child! She is the virginal, world-bearing primeval force, the sovereign lady, omnipotent Kali. In her is the stream of Ambrosia, of the indefinable Brahman. The indefinable nature of the world substance is the pledge of human freedom. Through her, we can take this substance with no properties of its own and shape it to our individual requirements.

Kundalini towers above the created universe. She has produced all the formative forces from the finest to the coarsest (the Tattwas). When she had produced the last of these, the Prithivi Tattwa, the formative force of solids, nothing more was left for her to do. She coils herself and "sleeps" in her final emanation, the earth principle, until her reawakening after "three-and-a-half times."[9] This prophecy could have been a reference to the Crucifixion, which took place three-and-a-half times after the Hindu epoch, and marked a turning point in history. Although Kundalini was thought to have a spiritual origin as heavenly fire, she came to earth in the creative process and turned into an earth goddess.

It should be clear by now, that Kundalini is the representative of the feminine, indeed of the eternal feminine. In contrast, Shiva as the begetter of the physical world is the eternal masculine. The aim of Kundalini Yoga is to reunite these two principles. The chief Tattwas are those of fire and light on the one hand, and of life and sound (the water element) on the other. They emanate from an earlier, uniform Tattwa, Akasha. More will be said about the Tattwas from time to time, when we come to speak of the individual chakras. This is just a brief outline of the subject. What we are after, according to the Tantric texts, is the union of Shiva and Shakti, in order to release the bound forces. Their union takes place on a rarefied plane, in the light, in the head region.

In the chakras, we will see three unions of the male and female principles. These unions begin at the lowest stage on the heavy plane of matter, where the will flows outward into desire. Their next meeting is on a higher plane in the Lotus of the heart (the 4th chakra), and their final one is in the Lotus of the head, in imponderable light. (See figures 2 and 5 on page 48, 70.) Europeans, too, pictured love in three guises or forms, when they came to conceptualize it: Eros, Philia and Agape—physical, mental, and spiritual love. Our earthly goal is to attain to spiritual love and to experience it in freedom.

---

[9] Seven is the number of time; so three-and-a-half is half a time.

The Four-Petaled
Lotus

The course of the spine is plotted by the other lotuses, but the Muladhara Chakra is its origin, lower end or root. The root of the spine lies in the center of this lotus, and hence it is called the "root-support," on the root chakra. Here the 72,000 *Nadis* (psychic nerves) are rooted. The ordinary nerves and their plexuses are simply the physical basis of the lotuses. The root lotus lies at the static pole of the body (See fig. 2 on page 48).

The root lotus closes the mouth of the spinal canal, so that a "boiler" (original image a goblet) is produced. In our present age it is filled with "lower astrality," with keen appetites that only the yogin governs, purifies, tames and arouses to the creative act.

Just as the coccyx consists of four obvious vertebrae, so this lotus has no more than four petals. They are colored crimson and each one bears a letter in gold. The letters are *Va*, *Śa* (palatal), *Sa* (cerebral) and *Sa*. Something will be said in a later chapter about the significance of the sounds in relation to the lotuses. We hope the reader will just accept the facts as stated for the time being, for we will discuss these sounds later. Va is at the top right of the diagram, and the letters move round in a circle.

The lotus encloses a light yellow square, from which eight spears radiate outward. Yellow is the color of earth; the square

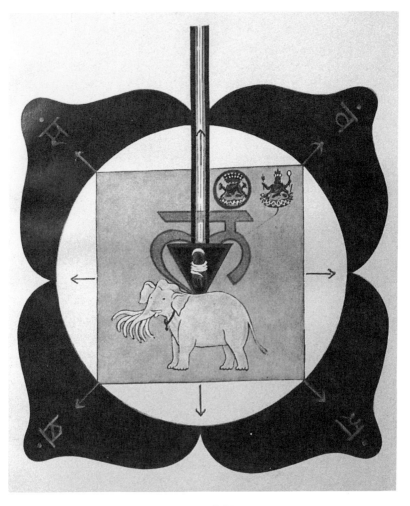

Figure 2. Muladhara chakra, the Four-petaled Lotus.

form is an expression of the Prithivi Tattwa. As already mentioned, the Tattwas are etheric formative forces. In the present instance, we are dealing with the fixed or earth etheric force—using the word earth in the sense given to it in the old doctrine of the elements. In modern spiritual science, Prithivi is called the Life Ether. As the picture shows, the root, seed or cause of the fixed or Life Ether, is expressed by the nasalized syllable *Lam*. It is concentrated in gleaming gold, and this life has its primary state in the sun. At one time it shone as the gold of inner wisdom. Thus, in a figurative manner, the golden solar life is causative of the fixed or earth state (Prithivi).

All things, as St. John the Evangelist said, were made by the Word. To the Westerner, this may seem like poetry; but to the yogin, the introduction to John's Gospel is an incontrovertible fact. Yogins know in practice that the individual is word made flesh. The word occurs everywhere in the lotuses at points of leverage for the cosmic forces of the spheres. The yogins regard this as a serious subject and can show, item by item, how the individual sounds—each according to its own nature—have created corresponding regions of the human body. The whole alphabet symbolizes the whole person.

The word *Lam*, which manifests itself in concentrated gold as the root or seed of the life in the Four-petaled Lotus, is a semivowel in Sanskrit. "And the Word was God," says John. The articulated sound embodies divinity, as our picture of the root lotus shows. The creative sound, in the form of a letter, is resting on the back of an animal. In this chakra, the animal is a white elephant, looking as it did when it rose out of the "Sea of Milk" of the universe. There is an old story in which the gods set the All in motion by churning this Sea.

The elephant is the bearer of the divinity. The different animals depicted in the lotuses are representative of the qualities of the formative forces (Tattwas) concerned. These are not terrestrial creatures, but astral ones, as perceived by seers. The fixity, solidity and firmness of the Life Ether is expressed here by the elephant.

So far, we have found an etheric (living) and an astral—animal (sentient) region in the lotus, plus the spiritual-creative word responsible for the coming into existence of the region.

On taking another look, we find something else—a god and a goddess! The deity can be viewed as the shared consciousness of everything gathered together in the lotus. The deity appears in both male and female form. In the cosmo-spiritual world, what is inner is female and what is outer is male, but this does not prevent a goddess from appearing outwardly as the powerful soul of the deity—which is polarized in manifestation.

The god in question is Brahma. He is shown with a white swanlike bird (again, this is not an earthly but an astrally observed creature). He is like a red-colored, four-faced, four-armed child, holding a rosary, staff and gourd. The goddess is a doorkeeper or "Dweller of the Threshold." She is the carrier of the "ever pure intelligence." She is stainless. To those who are enlightened, her character is Dweller of the Threshold. To the profane she only shows her wild and cruel side. She holds spears and a cultic sword, with which the sacrificial animal is slain.

But yogins learn that this sacrificial animal is none other than their own lower propensities, the lower astrality of the sexual passions. In the cauldron of the Root Lotus is Pandora's Box,[10] a witch's cauldron of unpurified animal drives and lusts. In her wild moods she shows her teeth. The goddess holds a bowl of wine, which inebriates fools, but turns into the heavenly wine of cosmic knowledge when drunk by yogins.

Students realize that it is only his or her own nature that is shown by this image. It meets each of us at the threshold. The sight is dismaying as long as it displays our hateful lower

---

[10] In Greek mythology, the source of all human ills. Angry over the theft of Heaven's fire by Prometheus, Jupiter gave Pandora this "booby-trapped" box, opened by her husband Epimetheus. *Tr.*

natures. When the soul's attitude changes, so does the Dweller's image.

Brahma's Dweller of the Threshold guards the doorway of the spirit. In more modern terms, this shows the student his or her own likeness. Yogins who have been purified, behold this wild, fierce deity as a clean, radiant, virginal being, whose heavenly side is forever unspotted.

Penned inside the female triangle is the male lingam, Shiva's phallus. They are in earthly communion, but have their opposite pole in the head, as we shall see, where their communion is in the light. The physical creative pole has its spiritual counterpart in the head. Out from the unity of the upper pole streams the creative power into the multiplicity of the lower pole, which then flows back to the spirit.

At the lower pole sleeps the earth goddess Kundalini, who guards the gateway that leads to Brahma, the creative deity. She is the world-bearing power that has given birth to everything. She is the world mother and nobody's child. When she had produced all types of form, and all the Tattwas also, there was nothing more for her to do but to coil herself up and go to sleep. Her name means *coiled*. Through her, the creative divine fire has entered the region of fixed earth. Heavenly power has become earthly, a heavenly goddess has become an earth goddess, a chthonic goddess. As such, she is the serpent. Her seat is in the Four-petaled Lotus, where celestial fire is fettered to mankind on earth. Like an entranced Cinderella, the heavenly power sits dreaming. In fact, if we look more closely, we shall see that it is divided into two sexes—but only for three-and-a-half times.

Three-and-a-half turns of glimmering light are coiled around the lingam. As an era, the Life Ether is assigned three-and-a-half times by the Hindus. Then comes the moment for it to be set free and elevated, so that the tree of life and the tree of knowledge can grow together again and fuse with one another.

Without this fundamental premise the aspirant can do nothing. The aim of yoga was and is to release ourselves from bondage, not for selfish reasons or to gain liberty for ourselves alone, but because those who have been liberated can benefit their brothers and sisters in the human race, and because if there were no initiates the world would perish. The higher spiritual realities are needed by the initiates. Kundalini is a spiritual light-organ which is carried in the darkness, where she rests in latency at the static pole of the individual. She is the mistress of that yoga that "frees those who know, and binds fools." She is also the grieving widow, because of her separation from the spiritual origin of the world. A latent power, she is dynamized by the Breath. Yogins awaken her and lead her up through the centers and into the region of the light of knowledge, where kundalini unites with the male force (Shakti) in order to conquer multiplicity.

The mantra used to awaken her is the word "I am"; in Sanskrit Hamsa (pronounced in a nasalized fashion as Hang-Sa). Hamsa or Hansa is also the word for swan (goose). This is why Brahma is shown with the swan. He meditates: "I am Brahma," "I am Spirit." The square where Brahma with the swan appears gives the content of meditation for those who can read it properly (see fig. 2 on page 48).

In meditating on Hamsa, yogins lead the latent light-force upward; then retain the breath—and with it the world-power—for a certain time. The breath is released while the mantra is being said backward: So ham or "I am that."

The world-music vibrates in the breath with the mantra, as the word travels over the sound ether (Apas). The meditation spiritually purifies the breath; the steady rhythm strengthens it and makes it healthy. From the left nostril the breath goes to Ida, and is expelled via the Pingala, and vice versa. Advanced students will be able to use the Sushumna once the coiled serpent has been raised. Then the breath can be brought from the naval to the crown of the head.

Each lotus petal contains a sound, and with it a divinity. In the four petals of the Muladhara Chakra there are three *S* sounds, or hissing sounds, and one *V* sound. The entire 50 letters of the Sanskrit alphabet are present in the 50 petals of the lotuses. Taken as a whole, each of us is an expression of the "world-word," present here in the astral centers but operative even in the physical body. As Rudolf Steiner once said: the complete alphabet is the complete person.

Now *H* is the spiritual sound, and we find it in the head. *S,* on the other hand, is a snake's sound, and we find it in the opposite, sexual, pole—here in the Four-petaled Lotus. For yogins, the spiritual *H* has a liberating effect on the earthly *S* of the imprisoned, divine creative power. Theme counterpoints theme in the four-leaved clover. Strindberg elaborated this in the "concealed door with the four-leaved trefoil" in *A Dream Play*.

The change that has taken place in the path of meditation in recent times is reflected in technique. Basically, the Westerner has a different constitution than has the Eastern person. The Westerner is much more interested in exercising the mind and the senses. Therefore it is much harder to practice true meditation, because sensory images and intellectual ideas act as a diversion. The Westerner tends to mistake intellect for spirit. Breathing exercises should be performed only under the guidance of a genuine teacher (guru), because there are hidden dangers involved. Correct meditation and a specific rhythm are vital. It makes a great deal of difference whether one retains the breath and the "world-force" after inhalation, or stops breathing for a few moments after exhalation and sends one's being into the circle of the earth. In some schools, yogins use their fingers to close all the gates of the senses during the held breath. But modern Westerners still like to give out their thoughts and impressions.

Even if errors in thinking occur, that is not as deleterious as letting the will take an improper direction. In the will, there is an opposition between good and evil, in the thoughts there is one between true and false, and in the feelings one between pleasant and unpleasant. The hazard of the upward path is the opportunity to slip into evil and to encourage destructive forces. The forces of the will are stronger than those of the intellect, but the inner light in turn absorbs and illuminates the dark forces of the will. These must first be recognized. Their point of origin is the consciousness pole in the head!

There are four regions in each chakra, which, although connected to the physical world, are interpenetrated by the Tattwas (etheric formative forces). The physical side is the actual site of the chakra in the body. The point through which the activities of the physical world stream in and out is in the lotus. A square represents the Tattwas concerned. Representing the astral side, we have an animal—in this case an elephant—that shows its specific quality. The lower Devachanic side is expressed by the seed-syllable *Lang*. The higher Devachanic side, which is consciously felt, is depicted by the god-goddess polarity. More specifically, it is the transition, or threshold, leading from one region to another.

In each Lotus there is a ladder, the rungs of which are for the meditator to climb. The combined imagery of the Lotus suggests the meditation by which the center can be awakened. Every creative activity descends from above to below, but the meditator traces the course of creation backward in order to achieve the desired union with the spiritual source.

On the other hand, the meditator can shake off passivity and act creatively, by working toward a wider objective than that of self-deliverance in the egoistic sense. "Be ye therefore perfect, even as your Father which is in heaven is perfect," is a challenge issued by Christ. "You are gods," He says. That means that the human being carries the seed of this possibility, thanks to divine grace. The initiate learns that the fate of the individual is indissolubly bound up with that of mankind.

Deliverance is meant for the many, not for the few. "As the rose smells, so smells the garden."

The Four-petaled Lotus serves as a gateway to the spiritual world, because its presence manifests itself in the physical-etheric-astral world of the body. The following descriptive verses have been written about Kundalini:

> She is the confounder of the world (she brings about Maya or illusion) by softly covering the mouth of Brahma-dvara with her own.

> Her brightness is like that of a flash of young, strong lightning. Her sweet murmur resembles the indistinct hum of a swarm of bees mad with love and the mellow cadence of sweet harmonious music.

> It is she who maintains all the beings of the world by means of inspiration and expiration, and shines in the cavity of the Root Lotus like a chain of brilliant lights.

It should be clearly understood that the Root Lotus is not grounded in the physical world, but in a "subtle region" as Avalon remarks.[11] He is talking about the human aura, which can be known from illustrations. Toward the lower part it loses its clarity, becomes indistinct and finally disappears in a haze. For the ancient Hindus, the lower world did not stop with mankind. Corresponding to the sevenfold heavenly world there was a sevenfold underworld called Patala. We stand in the middle between two worlds, in our own third world. Thus the Tantric texts speak of three worlds. These are telescoped into one another. I shall try to put this in modern terms.

During our earthly incarnation, the individual lives in the world of the senses. The higher, spiritual world is super-sen-

---

[11] Also see *The Serpent Power,* pp. 346 *ff.*

sual, and has a sub-sensual world as its counterpart. The individual dwells between that higher and this lower!

The insistence that the Root Lotus springs from below the physical world shows that it reaches down into the sub-sensual area. And this is where we find the great sources of danger. If someone concentrates on evil rather than good, it is entirely possible that he or she will slide down into the sub-sensual. Sufficient knowledge has been given to make a choice between the two. Many modern practices that rely on drugs to bend the mind lead to the sub-sensual region. Analysis also, if it goes into too many details, unravels the mind, splits the ego, and can bring someone to the edge of the sub-sensual.

At this point, I must point out the difference between the sexes in regard to the points of origin of the two Tattwic streams. In men they flow from the scrotum, and in women from the ovaries. These are the organs where the male and female hormones necessary for life are made. Now it is plain that the point of origin of the formative forces is lower in men than it is in women. This brings about a difference in nature. Men have descended into matter further than normal; women, on the other hand, do not stand completely on the earth. Only the middle between the two is the normal position for mankind.

Women can be said to be naturally closer to the supersensual, men to the sub-sensual; although the statement does need taking with a grain of salt, because there is a certain measure of femininity in every man and a certain measure of masculinity in every woman. But, putting such niceties to one side, let us trace the two streams of formative force flowing up the spine from their physical source. In the old texts, the stream from the left testicle is described as going to the left shoulder, twisting from there through the heart to the right shoulder and then on to the right nostril. The stream from the right testicle follows a route that mirrors this.

The reader will no doubt have guessed that the centers have a close connection with the endocrine glands and their production of hormones. The hormones, so essential to life, stand on the border between the etheric and the physical. So the chakras are clearly life-energy centers, specific control stations of the living formative forces (or Tattwas), without which physical, material bodies could not be animated. At the base of the spine there are actually gray and white brain cells in the terminal filament (filum terminale), but unlike what is found in the brain, the layers of gray cells are inside the layers of white. This highly sensitive substance is in communication with the Four-petaled Lotus—which underlines the importance of the latter to all living processes. In the sacral region we note the start of the spinal canal, which ascends all the way to the white matter of the brain.

The Six-Petaled
Lotus

This Svadhisthana chakra lies in the spinal center at the root of the genitals. Its six petals are colored vermilion. It contains six shining letters in the following order: *Ba, Bha, Ma, Ya, Ra, La*. There is also the "white region" of Varuna, a water region with the crescent as the form-tendency of the surface-building Apas Tattwa, the formative force of the liquid element. The crescent is surrounded by a white-leaved octagon as a geometric representation of the etheric formative force. In the middle of the lotus (Padma) we have the root force, the "seed" of the liquid Tattwa, the letter *Vang* or *V*. The *V* is the seed-syllable of water. (Everything liquid is called water in the old doctrine of the elements.)

Its active force is symbolized by a white makara, a kind of crocodile, that is to say, by a powerful animal living in the watery element. The god, or common consciousness of all that is comprised in this lotus, is Vishnu, with his scepter and mussel shell. He is yellow and youthful in appearance (thus no longer a child, like the god in the Four-petaled Lotus). This god is also the creative dot, the Bindu, out of which the "Word" proceeds to create the whole center. The word is seen descending into flesh from above to below. (See fig. 3 on page 60.)

Above is the creative dot in divine consciousness, below is the power of the word, which creates the region by means

Figure 3. Svadhisthana chakra, the Six-petaled Lotus.

of a third entity, the animal or the astral desire. A fourth element is the particular ether (or Tattwa), the architect of the physical. From the divine consciousness emanates force (energy), the word, the goddess; general movement arises out of will-power or fire. Out of this, in turn, arises the specific movement, the seed of a definite word. This stirs up desire on arriving in the astral sphere (animal): it wants to be (desire). Further down it becomes etheric; the specific formative tendency appears; here is the crescent, with the octagon—made of two squares—as a two-sex sign. The outwardly turned leaves are a picture of the Whole as they issue from the position of the lotus in the body. Etheric streams flow from the leaf-tips.

When the yogin awakens and guides it, the threefold stream of kundalini fire—bringing with it the power of perception—rises through the centers of the spine. The latent force then becomes dynamic. There is a connection between the lotus we are now considering and the Thousand-petaled Lotus—the crown chakra. From the latter, so we are told, drops the nectar that intoxicates the Shakti (world force) Rakini who dwells in the region of the Six-petaled Lotus. The intoxication refers to an impaired state of consciousness. Six passions are associated with the six petals—lust, anger, greed, deceit, pride and envy.

Meditation releases the student from this negativity and makes everything positive. Body, soul and spirit, or, in other words, the senses, emotions, and thoughts, have to be brought into harmony with one another, too. The longings are extinguished from within outward, not by external means such as flagellation. Only an inner renunciation can overcome the thirst of the appetites (the astral animality in individuals). In order to cultivate this lotus, the student must be completely governed by the self-consciousness. Then union is possible with beings of a higher type in so far as their presence is felt in the spirit world.

The Ten-Petaled
Lotus

The seat of the Manipura chakra is also in the spine, in the region of the fifth lumbar vertebra. It is also called the Navel Lotus because of the proximity to the navel of the ganglionic center known as the solar plexus, which is found on the aorta just under the diaphragm. The solar plexus is in the pit of the stomach in immediate contact with the Ten-petaled Lotus. All initiates recognize this center as a lower brain. It was the prototype of the sympathetic nerve plexus generally. (See fig. 4 on page 64.)

The petals have the color of heavy-laden rain clouds. In each petal there appears a blue letter: *Da* (cerebral), *Dha, Na, Ta, Tha, Da, Dha, Na, Pa, Pha.* In the center is a fiery red triangle with its apex pointing downward. On each side of the triangle is a swastika—simply as an expression of mobility.[12] It represents the formative force of fire, the Tejas Tattwa.

The red seed-syllable of Fire is the sound *Rang* (R). This is in the sphere of inspiration. In the astral sphere of the imagination, the sound becomes Ram, which is Lord of Fire in the animal-related astral world. In the intuitive sphere of consciousness, and above the red triangle, we see the ancient

---

[12] The swastika originally was an Eastern symbol that was used (and misunderstood) by the Nazis.

Figure 4. Manipuraka chakra, the Ten-petaled Lotus.

"Ruddy One," the storm-god Rudra riding a bull daubed with white ashes. He wields thunder and lightning, as images of the nerve and blood processes. Beside him is a goddess, the manifestation of his power. She appears in blue, and is wearing precious stones and pearls. The chakra itself is known as Manipura, because it shines like a jewel. The female figure is goddess of the digestive center, the fundamental strength of animal nourishment. This center is the brain of the digestive process. She is realistically shown dripping in fat and gore. In the red god and the blue goddess, there are hidden the secrets of red and blue blood. From the lower pole up to and including this point, the divinities of meditation are "flesh-eaters." In other words, they represent spiritual processes present in animal nutrition but concealed from normal consciousness.

In the higher centers, this is no longer the case. By thinking along these lines, we can find meaning in the gruesome, bloodthirsty gods and goddesses of the old cults. We can see them as phenomena actually present in ourselves, as cosmic powers and cosmic consciousness that descend creatively into our human regions and become chthonic. Nothing has changed because, even today, the physical and energy bodies have to be resigned in sleep to obscure cosmic forces.

The goddess is intoxicated with Ambrosia. This indicates that indulgence in animal foods does not result in complete lucidity and soberness. The yogin avoids such foods. But, in general, Ambrosia is solid food, which is proper for the life-pole in the lower being, and is carried upward by the kundalini fire. Nectar, on the other hand, has to do with the fluid of illumination that drops down from the sphere of consciousness, from the Soma Chakra in the head. The female Ida channel contains nectar, too.

Ambrosia is related to the Prithivi and Apas Tattwas (life and sound), nectar to the Vayu and Tejas Tattwas (light and heat). They are terms reminiscent of milk and honey, or bread and wine. They ascend and descend, as the case may be, into the chalice of the heart (of the Twelve-petaled Lotus) and act as upper and lower reference points for the hub of existence.

The bull powdered with white ash, on which the god Rudra sits, must also be understood in connection with the digestive processes, in which part of the food becomes residue or ash. The bull itself is the productive aspect of the digestive powers.

Meditation on this center gives the yogin an awareness of the forces that create, sustain and destroy the universe. He or she discovers the same forces in this region. Another discovery is the relationship between this lotus and the sense of sight, which is sharpened for the perception of shape and color. On the other hand, there is the affinity of the Six-petaled Lotus with the sense of taste (water region). Tasting liberates the elemental essence from its fixed state (Prithivi). For example, the power of the Sun is trapped in the solid substance of a plant, but the whole elemental circuitry that led to the solid state can be put into reverse. The elemental spirit is released like the human spirit when it leaves the physical body at death.

Speaking of Prithivi (life ether, and the cause of solidity) in the root center, yoga doctrine tells us that this has an affinity with the sense of smell. It was Steiner who first explained the nature of the relationship. Just as taste is at the pole opposite to the organic process of becoming solid, so smell is at the pole opposite to the process of disintegration by burning. Floating in each whiff of scent, are odor "shadows" like disembodied spirits. Even putrefaction is a form of slow, low-temperature combustion. The burning ends in ash (Shiva).

What, then, does yoga doctrine mean by associating the sense of sight with the region of the navel lotus? Here again, we have to consider the polarity involved—this time, the polarity of seeing and digesting.

In seeing, an image of something is impressed on the eye from outside. Delicate nerves lead inward from the eye and carry the image to the brain and from the brain to the mind. Seeing "puts us in the picture." In contrast to this, the digestive process has to do with essence rather than image. Metabolism is a matter of reality not of representation. Since it is polar to the act of vision, the act of digestion works outward from the inside.

Just as thinking leads to the discharge of ideas, so digestion leads to evacuation and elimination. Rudolf Steiner alluded to the polarity character in various lectures. It was these that first opened my eyes to the profound meaning of yoga teaching in regard to the sense affinities of the chakras. Now the spiritual elements extracted from the flow of nutrition during the process of digestion ascend with the blood through the heart to the brain. There they prepare the groundwork for the thoughts and ideas. With the help of the pancreas and gall bladder, they are separated from their physical dross and are absorbed by the bloodstream. The brain tissues are replenished by the blood and revitalized by the breath.

During the process of thinking, so Steiner informs us, a fine secretion takes place in the glandular system. The content of thought is connected with (and exerts an influence on) the functioning of the glands. In the act of remembering, that is to say, in the reproduction of images, the formative forces (Tattwas) of the glands are evoked.

By meditating on the Navel Lotus, the student learns conscious control of sense impressions. Instead of being at the mercy of unexplained sympathies and antipathies, he or she learns to make deliberate associations. Arbitrary effects and illusions are overcome. What had form and fire now gains light and color. Various forces and hidden qualities of nature are unveiled as the student learns to recognize the actual role played by nature (animal, vegetable, metal, mineral) in her various kingdoms. Atmospheric phenomena are seen in their proper light. The auric colors of living things become visible to the yogin, revealing their characteristics and talents.

As long as the external senses have the upper hand, the lotus has no say. The flow of unconscious memories will lead from illusion to illusion until all the sense impressions arriving from outside have been brought under control. What wells up from below, from the earth, from the chthonic powers, by virtue of the process of digestion, enters the blood stream and becomes progressively etherealized in the region above the diaphragm, where the breath unites with the blood. Spiritualization is as much a part of reality as the material side of things is.

The Twelve-Petaled
Lotus

The Anahata Chakra is the lotus of the cardiac region, called the heart chakra or 4th chakra. Its petals are light red, with twelve darker red letters in them. In the middle of the lotus is a grayish hexagram (the gray smoke of fire, which gave birth to time and is the spiritual basis of life). The hexagram is composed of two interpenetrating triangles: one pointing upward, the other pointing down. It is the sign of the macrocosm, because this can be experienced in the heart. The region has also been experienced as that of the Vayu Tattwa (light). The ancient Hindus still saw light and fire as a pair. Because of its fleetness, the gazelle or antelope is the astral animal of this element. In the lower Devachanic region, the word *yang* (*Υ*) sounds out as the spiritual name like a concentrated extract of dark smoke. (See fig. 5 on page 70.)

All the spiritual seed-syllables of the four Tattwas are semivowels. *L* (*la, lang*) is the seed of Prithivi; *V* (*va, vang*) is the seed of Apas; *R* (*ra, rang*) is the seed of Tejas; *Υ* (*ya, yang*) is the seed of Vayu.

The element of consciousness in the lotus is the three-eyed lord, Isha, astride a black antelope (black being the dull color of the spirit) and wielding a primitive type of shepherd's crook. He is the sovereign of the three lower centers, which are so strongly involved with metabolism and with our animal nature.

Figure 5. Anahata chakra, the Twelve-petaled Lotus.

From here, Isha rules the lower powers with his staff. The staff creates order, in the same way as the ego in humans and sunlight in the universe should do. Next to him is the goddess enthroned on a red lotus. She is golden colored and saffron robed, and wears jewels and garlands of bones.

From time to time, the goddess makes gestures to drive away fear: "Fear not" is the first lesson for the seer to learn. We come across gestures in all the lotuses. I have deliberately refrained from going into these. By the term *mudras,* we understand certain gestures and positions of the hands and fingers, such as are common to religions everywhere. One of the things they do is to direct the life currents into various channels.[13]

Here we touch the domain of magic, on which opinions vary widely today. It is utterly rejected by some, especially by those who do not know what it is. Certainly Faust's verdict was that it would have been better for him if he had withdrawn from its path. But Faust lived in the Middle Ages when a great struggle for knowledge took place and old conventions were being broken. Knowledge was being obtained by thinking and observation; magic, on the other hand, belonged to the dark human depths of will and vital energy, most strongly evident in the blood processes.

The time is now ripe to resume the study of the real processes that go on in living things. To the extent that we succeed in uniting the trees of knowledge and life, science and magic will join forces on the plane of moral good. We still have a long way to go before this can happen, but at least we ought to be taking the first steps in that direction. A knowledge of the higher laws of living things will turn us into discerning magicians. Magic is Kriyashakti, or solar power. The recognition of this fact removes the bad odor from the word. "Fear

---

[13] For practical instructions on this topic see "Therapeutic Mudras," by Dr. C. P. Mehra, in *Yoga Today* magazine for December 1983 and January 1984. *Tr.*

not," say the mudras (gestures) of the Heart Lotus. This admonition is also addressed to those who think it appropriate to investigate the life forces in a spirit of superstitious awe.

Whereas the deity in the Ten-petaled Lotus is drunk with Ambrosia, the goddess in the Twelve-petaled Lotus seems to be assuaged by the nectar dripping from the pole of inner light in the head.

At the very center of the lotus is a golden female triangle with the male token inside it, along with a lunar crescent that serves as a basin to catch the nectar. This imagery also depicts the lambent soul. The soul burns here like an eternal, steady, inextinguishable flame. It shines like 10,000 suns in a windless place, uninfluenced from outside. Reposing in itself it is Atma. A picture, this, of the famous "ever-burning lamp."

The center is called Anahata because it is the foundation of the cosmic word. The letter Y gives birth to it—a semi-vowel lying half-way between the vowel I and the consonant J. Yahweh, Jesus, and I, are formed from it. The word is born here without the intervention of two things. The birth by the word is a true immaculate conception in this region of Anna! Anna means grace; Anael is the gracious God. Here is the altar of grace in humans. Our verses say of this lotus: "Meditate in it concerning the seat of grace."

Below the Twelve-petaled Lotus is a still smaller Eight-petaled red Lotus, which belongs to the cardiac region and can actually be glimpsed within it. It is a subsidiary organ containing a jeweled altar with a sheltering roof or canopy. Here stands the sacred trees of the sacred grove. This is the inner shrine of a spiritual worship of God; a worship which must be performed in the heart.

In the Twelve-petaled Lotus is the region of the Voice of Silence, where the harmony of the sun and the spheres is heard. The divine reveals itself here in the inner word. Light and word (sound), Vayu and Apas, work together. The heart organ is the place where the individual lights the spiritual light organ from the outside. By means of the heart, the higher ego uses the physical self as a tool. The former manipulates the latter through the heart.

What has form in the Sixteen-petaled Lotus shows in the Twelve-petaled Lotus as the characteristic of psychic warmth and coldness. That which tends to growth and development radiates psychic warmth, and that which rests on wasting away and destruction radiates psychic coldness.

The meditating yogin gains a deep understanding of natural processes. To awaken the Twelve-petaled Lotus, he or she needs mainly to have complete control of the internal dialogue. There are six virtues that are helpful here:

1) The interpretation of incoming impressions in a symbolic or analogical way. Logical thought is consecutive.

2) Control of the actions. They incorporate consecutiveness.

3) Training in perseverance.

4) Tolerance—the ability to put oneself in someone else's position and to have understanding for all. The sun shines on all alike!

5) Confidence, faith and receptiveness for everything; the student must become open to all the experiences of life.

6) The keeping of a sense of proportion in life—a balanced attitude in all conditions of life.

The Eight-petaled Lotus, which is so closely associated with the Twelve-petaled Lotus, is connected with the center of the heart. It has various quickly-changing forms and colors, and is shining and opalescent. Streams of shapes and colors flow out from it to the whole astral body. The most important go to the chakras, traverse the petals and regulate their whirling. From the tips of the petals they then move out into space.

More spiritually developed people have larger auric enve-
lopes. The currents flow in directly to the Twelve-petaled Lotus. There are streams flowing upward to the Sixteen-petaled
and Two-petaled Lotuses, others are flowing downward. The
heart organ is very important for spiritual and occult development. Peach blossom is the ground-color of the vital body.

When the objective spiritual world with its great secrets
(miracles) gains access to the inner citadel of the heart, that is
the beginning of what the true yogin means by "liberation."
Liberation, in this sense, is very different than our desire for
freedom.

Yoga doctrine also sees a relationship between the Twelve-
petaled Lotus and the sense of touch. The organ of this sense
is the skin, which covers the entire periphery of the body. Thus
touch is, indeed, the most peripheral of the senses. Its opposite
pole is a centering activity in the heart. The ego is like the
center of the circle.

The Sixteen-Petaled Lotus

The Vishuddha Chakra is located at the base of the throat in the spinal center of the neck region. The shade of the petals is smoky, and they carry sixteen purple letters, fourteen of which are vowels and two of which are aspirates, so that this Lotus has been called the vocal organ. It is called the throat or 5th chakra. (See fig. 6 on page 76.)

Here is the center of Akasha, or the fifth ether; which really is the first ether, because the others—already familiar to us—take their origin from it. Rudolf Steiner pointed out that the chemical or sound ether (Apas)—which we nowadays think of as a uniform entity—was regarded as twofold by the Hindus. The pure sound ether was in Akasha. Therefore this center was known as the great purity center—Vishuddha. Another name for it is Bharatisthana (the god of speech).

Here is the sphere of the purified soul—the gate of the great liberation. The soul has been purified through the perception of Hangsah, the inner spiritual forces of the Sun (Hang) and of the Moon (Sah); in other words, through the perception of the cosmic and divine forces at work in human affairs.

So far, we have encountered triangles four times; three having the apex pointing downward and one having the apex pointing upward. All these triangles were colored. The fifth

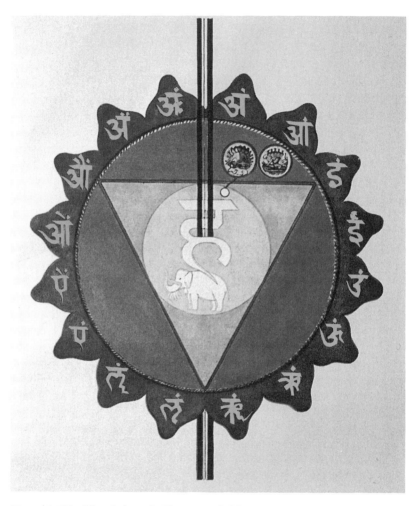

Figure 6. Visuddha chakra, the Sixteen-petaled Lotus.

triangle appears here, and it is white, being perfectly pure and full of refined spirituality.

Within the purified receptive female triangle appears the spherical form of the Akasha Ether. It looks like a white full moon without stains or shadows—that is to say, without a man in the moon (hare in the moon). The astral side of things is represented by a white elephant. The tendency to heaviness, to solidity, to "becoming flesh," is already present in this primordial ether, in the sphere of the word. It builds forms; the cosmic memory lives in it, in the Akasha. The meditating student is enabled to perceive forms and even personal incarnations. The three states of the world—what was, what is, and what will be—are revealed to the seer. The mental cause of what appears astrally in the elephant, is the spiritual sound "Hang," or *H*.

The common center of consciousness takes the form of Shiva, who is androgynous here. The left side of his body is golden, the right side is white. He is placed on the golden lion throne, his feet rest on a bull. The goddess next to him is sitting on a lion. It is said that she is half of Shiva's body, the mother of the universe from whom everything has emerged. She is "purer than the ocean of nectar, which is fresh and white."

The androgyne and the use of the bull and lion for the male and female indicate (besides other aspects) the future significance of this organ. The larynx will be transformed so that it can produce the human form through the word. The word was at one time with God; it has been handed over to human beings and is ready to bring forth. In any case, this is the region of speech. The word is voiced from the throat (kantha, in Sanskrit).

Yoga doctrine informs us that our speech is merely the fourth stage, or fourth metamorphosis, of the word. The mysteries know of four types of form (rounds) that the earth has gone through so far:

the formless (Arupa), higher Devachan (spirit),
the formed (Rupa), lower Devachan (spirit),
the astral, astral world (soul),
the physical,

the last of which is condensed astral stuff, and what we are now living in.

The following technicalities may be skipped if the reader prefers, but for those who are interested, we would mention that the Hindus recognize four exactly comparable types of form in the world of sound. Unmanifest sound, in which only the wish to utter something is present, is the first condition. This unmanifest matrix, the mother-form of sound, lies sleeping as a basic force in the Four-petaled Lotus.

The wish and desire to speak proceed from those regions in which cosmic and human forces come in contact. Here speech is motionless. The urge to speak causes the basic force of speech to ascend to a higher level. The second condition occurs as nothing more than general motion. We are told that it is linked with Manas, so that the light of cosmic intelligence is active in this general motion. This second condition is produced by a rise from the Four-petaled Lotus through the Six-petaled Lotus and as far as the Ten-petaled Lotus.

From there, upward through the heart, the condition of speech is connected with the Buddhi element and receives life, adopts a special motion, acquires a special type of gesture, and is condensed in the Etheric. The life spirit produces the gesture. This is the third condition.

In the next stage, the inner sound is first capable of being heard by others; it is manifested and has an exact articulation. This is the part that is brought about by the processes between the heart and the larynx.

Between the larynx and the Two-petaled Lotus in the region of the forehead, there is produced that power of speech (Sanskrit: *vak,* Latin: *vox*) that provides a precise vehicle for the etheric inner sound ascending from the heart. In the interplay of above and below, we have the birth of the fourth condition of speech, namely the form of words we use. The etheric-living impulse slips inside the fixed form in which it can be heard by those with whom we wish to communicate. This sort of speech is called the "very hard," Vaikhari, by the yogins.

The unfolding of human speech can be likened to that of a plant:

> in the Four-petaled Lotus it germinates;
> in the Six-petaled Lotus, the nodes and
>   leaf-buds are formed;
> in the Ten-petaled Lotus we have the leaves;
> in the Twelve-petaled Lotus, the flower-buds appear;
> in the Sixteen-petaled Lotus come the flowers.

It is extraordinarily interesting to study the arrangement of the sounds on the lotus petals. They have to be read clockwise. From top to bottom we can trace the order of the Sanskrit alphabet. "The whole human being is the whole alphabet." It becomes obvious from the lotuses how the cosmic word has operated in a specific way in the human centers.

The head, center of ideas, is an exception, because it contains all 50 sounds twenty times over. The phonetic arrangement of the sounds in the Sanskrit alphabet is produced by the position of the astral-etheric centers, which were first created from the sounds. The series of letters starts with the gutturals, in which the sound is trapped between the back of the tongue and the soft palate.

Next come the palatals, where the middle of the back of the tongue is pressed against the hard palate. These are followed by the linguals (or cerebrals), in which the tip of the tongue is bent back to touch the highest part of the palate. Then we have the dentals, in which the tip of the tongue makes contact with the teeth. After these come the labials or lip sounds, in which the upper and lower lips work together, or else the lower lip and the upper teeth are involved.

There are five sounds in each of the five groups: tenues (hard and voiceless); aspirated tenues (the same but aspirated); mediae (voiced and soft); aspirated mediae (the same aspirated); nasals. This arrangement appears, at first sight, to be the result of careful study and logical thought. However, it is really a result of the creative word itself. Human effort has done no more than copy cosmic intelligence.

In addition to these five groups, we have (next in order) a sixth, comprising four semivowels, which, so we saw, were related to the four types of Ether. The seventh group has three sibilants: a palatal, cerebral and dental S.

The aspirate H, on its own, forms an eighth group. This sound, called Ha, brings the number of letters minus vowels to thirty-three. Thirty-three is the number of the Vedic deities and also of the vertebrae in the human spine (if one includes the four fused vertebrae of the coccyx). The eighth group, with its sound Ha, is represented in the highest part of the body, the head, where it starts the alphabet by taking precedence over the Ka-sound of the first group.

Now, think for a moment of our own alphabet. This starts with A and ends with Z. The A comes from the Aleph (or alef) of the Western Semitic alphabet, which was pronounced with a slight aspiration. This was the H.[14] The Z, of course, is a sibilant. In the sounds A and Z, therefore, there is a clear echo of the polarity between the Sanskrit H and S—and so of the

---

[14] Strictly speaking, the Aleph is not an aspirate, but a glottal stop. H is represented in the Semitic alphabet by the letter Heth. However, if one thinks of a Hebrew Aleph and the Sanskrit Ha as sharing a certain throatiness, it is perhaps possible to see a tenuous link between them. Our letter A came quite naturally from Aleph because, in addition to its normal use as a glottal stop, Aleph also had the secondary role of a vowel letter standing for the A-sound. *Tr.*

great polarity between the head and genital regions, lettered as we have seen with *H* and *S*. Incidentally, the Western Semitic alphabet, besides being the source of our Latin alphabet, is also related to Hieroglyphics.

The polarities just mentioned are really a reflection of the polarity between Heaven and Earth. Now the head is responsible for speech in its fourth condition, and it molds the etheric-astral stream of incipient sound welling up from the genitals to the throat. Form, force and feeling meet in the head.

The sound-letters start with *Ka* in the Twelve-petaled Lotus. This, the Lotus of the Heart region, contains five gutturals, five palatals and two cerebrals, from *Ka* through the cerebral *Tha*. It should be noted that when the Sanskrit cerebrals are transliterated into Latin type, the same signs are employed for them as for the dentals, except that they have an additional dot placed underneath.

The Ten-petaled Lotus contains all the dentals and two labials. The Six-petaled Lotus begins with *Ba* and has three semivowels as well. The Four-petaled Lotus has the last semivowel and the three sibilants. Interestingly enough, the Hebrew letter Shin is shaped like three tongues, corresponding to the three currents that rise in the spine through kundalini. Aleph was the first letter of the Western Semitic alphabet and looks something like the knot formed by the channels of psychic energy in the frontal region at the root of the nose. This is how one should derive the forms of the sounds as they originally were: from supersensual astral-etheric realities and not from what is perceived by the senses.

The vowels occur exclusively in the vocal or laryngeal organ. In the ordinary Sanskrit there are thirteen vowels, nine of which are simple and four of which are double or diphthongs: the nine simple vowels: *a, ā, i, ī, u, ū, ri, rī, li* (short and long as marked), and the four diphthongs: *e* (from *a* and *i* pronounced together quickly), *ai, o* (from *a* and *u*), *au*. In addition to these thirteen, we have a long *lī,* bringing the tally of simple vowels to ten. Finally, two aspirated vowels, *Ang* and *Ah* complete the sixteen vowels of the Sixteen-petaled Lotus.

The vowels form a contrast to the consonant vortices. They represent a middle, psychic element between the two poles: the thirty-two (2 × 16) sounds below the throat and the 1001 sounds of the head—the twenty-times-fifty of the Thousand-petaled Lotus plus the separate *H* in the Two-petaled Lotus. The polarity between the *H* or *K* and the *S* is expressed in Greek by avoiding Scylla and falling into Charybdis.[15]

From *Ka* through the dental *Ta* (fourth petal in the Ten-petaled Lotus) we have the first sixteen sounds. From *Tha* through the dental *Sa* of the Four-petaled Lotus, we have the second sixteen sounds. The sixteen vowels form a third series. The three series taken together form the "divine triangle." The runic Futhark (or the primitive Germanic alphabet) also has three rows, three generations. The vowels belong to Brahma, the next line from *Ka* through *Ta* to Vishnu (Son), the third line from *Tha* through *Sa* to Shiva (as lord of all creatures). Inside the triangle shines the divine eye, contemplating what the word has created in the world.

The following are the letters in the lotuses:

In the 2-petaled: *Hang, Kschang*
In the 16-petaled: *Ang, Āng, Ing, Īng, Ung, Ūng, Ring, Rīng, Lring, Lrīng, Eng, Aing, Ong, Aung, Āng, Āh*

---

[15] Scylla is a rock on the Italian side of the straits of Messina and Charybdis is a whirlpool on the opposite Sicilian coast. Homer, Horace and Shakespeare all refer to them. They were a notorious danger to shipping. The polarity here, it should be noted, is between left and right, not between upper and lower. *Tr.*

In the 12-petaled: *Kang, Khang, Gang, Ghang, Nyang, Chang, Chang, Jang, Jhang, Nyang, Tang, Thang*

In the 10-petaled: *Dang, Dhang, Nang, Tang, Thang, Dang, Dhang, Nang, Pang, Phang*

In the 6-petaled: *Bang, Bhang, Mang, Yang, Rang, Lang*

In the 4-petaled: *Vang, Shang, Shang, Sang.*

All told, this comes to 50 letters. But there is a subsidiary fifty-first letter, the Vihara, an aspirate *H* pronounced like the Scottish ch in "loch." This is located in the head.

Phonetic classifications of the letters are as follows:

	Tenues	Aspirated tenues	Mediae	Aspirated mediae	Nasals
Gutterals:	*ka*	*kha*	*ga*	*gha*	*na*
Palatals:	*ca* (tscha)	*cha*	*ja* (dscha)	*jha*	*ña*
Cerebrals:	*ṭa*	*ṭha*	*ḍa*	*ḍha*	*ṇa*
Dentals:	*ta*	*tha*	*da*	*dha*	*na*
Labials:	*na*	*pha*	*ba*	*bha*	*ma*

Plus:

4 Semivowels: *ya, ra, la, va*

3 Sibilants: *śa,* (palatal), *ṣa* (sha, cerebral), *sa* (dental)

1 Aspirate: *ha*

This amounts to 33 sounds.

In addition there are 13 or 16 vowels. The three in brackets are not ordinarily included:

Simple: *ā, a, i, ī, u, ū, r, ṝ, ḷ, (ḹ)*

Diphthongs: *e, ai, o, au, (āng, āh)*

The short *e* is a diphthong because it is formed from *a* and *i*, and the *o* is a diphthong because it is formed from *a* and *u*.

True and meaningful thoughts assist the Sixteen-petaled Lotus to unfold. Eight of its petals were developed in ancient times, they are natural phenomena. The remaining eight have to be developed by each of us as individuals. The process is assisted by instructions such as those given by Gautama Buddha to his disciples in the Eightfold Path:

1) through right belief (paying attention to having the correct notions);

2) through right resolve (right decision-making);

3) right speech (thoughtful and considerate);

4) right life (natural and spiritual);

5) right action (in harmony with one's environment);

6) right desire (to fulfil one's duties);

7) right thought (viewing one's experiences in the right light after passing them before one);

8) right self-absorption (pondering on the purpose and content of one's life).

Through the consciousness of the Sixteen-petaled Lotus one becomes aware of forms, as I have already said. The laws governing natural phenomena appear in animated forms. Each thought has an appropriate form. For example, resentful thoughts are barbed, kindly thoughts are like open flowers;

clear thoughts are regular and symmetrical, unclear thoughts have wavy outlines (according to Steiner). "This region is the gateway to the Great Liberation for those who seek the wealth that is in Yoga, with pure thoughts under control," says the thirtieth verse.

The Two-Petaled
Lotus

All cognitive impulses proceed from the brightly shining center known as the Two-petaled Lotus, or the Ajna Chakra. Its name, which means command, instruction, precept, implies as much. It is situated approximately three-quarters of an inch behind the forehead between the eyebrows, and is called the 6th chakra or the third eye. (See fig. 7 on page 88.)

Some Indian yogins start their development, not from the Four-petaled Lotus, but from above, from the Two-petaled Lotus. They are the Gayatri-Sadhakas, whose chief meditation is the Sun-stanza of the Rig Veda (III, 62:10). Professor H. Beckh's translation reads:

> The love-inspiring light of the All-vivifier,
> of the Divine Solar Being, is what (in our meditation)
> we wish to absorb; it gives us the incentive to
> engage in (completely devout) thought.

We now come to a fact that is very significant for the age in which we live. In a world of individual lives everything has its hour, as the Bible intimates. Only in the "One Undivided Life" does outer time return to the inner essence of time. In the stream of events, the life bestowed by God runs into the external world and produces development in humankind and in the cosmos.

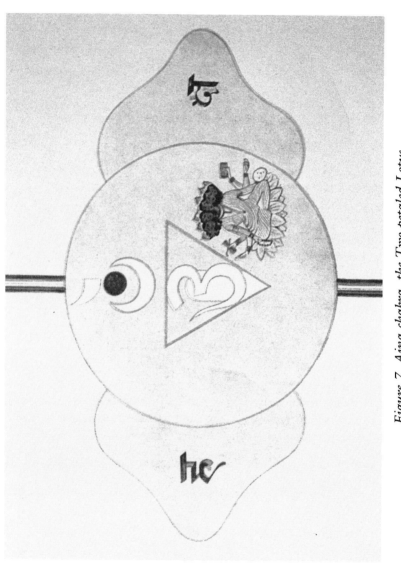

Figure 7. Ajna chakra, the Two-petaled Lotus.

It is essential for the meditator to treat consciousness, not as a fixed, but as a variable quantity. Many steps lead from a darkened to an ever more luminous state of consciousness. From trance, the course of development leads through dreamless sleep to dream, and from dream to the currently normal condition of waking, reflecting consciousness.

As the Buddha admonished his disciples: *"To be awake, you monks, is everything."* The transition from one state of consciousness to another is not made by merging. If that were so, there would be no stages, no clear distinctions. There are breaks between the stages that are pointers to the spiritual. The stages reveal to us specific cesuras in the creation of the kingdoms of human beings and the world. The Hindus formed a clear picture of the creation of the world. When Brahma breathes out, a world is born; when he breathes in, the world disappears, because it is taken back by the creative god.

Appearance alternates with Disappearance in an eternal rhythm. Everything that comes into being is subject to the law of re-dissolution. On issuing from the spiritual world, the will of the divinity condenses into life and light, to the sensation of life and to consciousness, to the realization of the ethical through the created human being. From the condensation a reaction takes place in the shape of relaxation and dissolution as Brahma breathes the world in again until, finally, all is dispersed into the spiritual world from which the visible universe emerged. Our spiritual part shares both in the visible physico-material world and also in the spiritual world which is at present invisible to us.

The human spirit also participates in the "One Undivided Life" in the divinity. The spiritual side of the individual becomes immersed in the visible world at birth and retires from it bearing the quintessence of its experiences. Life in this world alternates with life in the spiritual world, where the student "dines with the gods." Now, the rhythm of becoming and passing away does not result in a state of "eternal equilibrium" as Nietzsche contended. The operation of the divine breath allows for development associated with the raising of consciousness.

Take, for instance, the natural realm. A mineral, or rock, has no consciousness, or so most people would say. However, those who are spiritually awakened know that it is not without a degree of consciousness. We could perhaps say that the rock is in the lowest state, and stands as if it were in a trance. Plants sleep, and animals dream. Only mankind has advanced far enough to be able to wake and think. Since the kingdoms of nature are clearly distinct—that is to say, they do not merge—and since they exhibit different degrees of consciousness, it is possible to see the dividing lines between them as representative of those breaks between creations, in which fragmented life is withdrawn into the unfragmented life of the undivided divinity, into "Pralaya," or the period of rest from creation. When creation is resumed, the old stages reappear, but with the addition of a higher, new stage.

No one who has come to accept the law of "dying and becoming" can possibly think that the state of consciousness we have now reached is the last one open to us. It has to be admitted that higher states of consciousness are theoretically possible, and personal experience substantiates them. Of course, there is no other evidence besides personal experience, but meditation is able to place the evidence in our hands. It allows us to rise to states of spiritual awareness, the reality of which we can check for ourselves, giving us expanded points of view, and a knowledge of the world and of what it conceals in its innermost core. Everything is undergoing metamorphosis and is in a process of change and development. Our own spiritual lives and mental abilities unfold according to this law by the will of the Creative Powers. Therefore it is important that students traveling along the road to knowledge set out from the correct stage of consciousness when seeking to go higher.

This is why the Indian school of Gayatri-Sadhakas starts from the light pole of the human ego, not from the dark pole. The spiritual, higher ego is creatively at work in the metabolic processes of the lower individual. But people are not conscious here at present; they are conscious only in the upper pole, in the head and thought processes.

Meditation is hard work. We read of the historical Buddha, who left his earthly shell ca. 480 B.C., that it was under the Bo-tree, the tree of knowledge (or Bodhi), that he first reached that depth of meditation in which he developed the forehead lotus. One result of this was the appearance of the jewel in the forehead known as the "urna." It is the spirit that builds the body for itself! So the "jewel in the lotus" took physical form in him in this way.

On turning from Asia to see what was happening at that time in Greece, then the cultural center of Europe, we find that a revolution was occurring in the spiritual life of humanity. The interfusion of the human soul with the external world of nature and the elements was becoming a thing of the past.

The intellectual processes were emancipated from feeling and willing, and the original unity of thinking, feeling and willing began to fall apart into three. Up to this time, thinking had been part of feeling, and people knew what it was to be wise. But now the ancient wisdom flickered toward extinction as thought became more abstract. Men and women were increasingly thrown back on their own resources as the guiding, teaching and initiating divine world receded from view. Previously, the supernatural had been taken for granted and had been particularly real to the thinking feelings. But now the intercourse with gods and elementary beings had ceased, and men and women saw themselves as all alone in the world. This development has continued right down to our own day and age, because people today still feel isolated and godforsaken. At the time of which we have been speaking, Protagoras (480–410 B.C.) uttered the famous words:

"Man is the measure of all things,
of things that are that they are,
and of things that are not that they are not."[16]

And the Delphic oracle admonished:

"Know thyself."

Plato (427–347 B.C.) still believed in the existence of what he called Ideas, external to the soul and interwoven with the cosmos. These were the realities we needed to grasp and understand. For Aristotle (384–322 B.C.), however, ideas existed only in the mind. The illusion (call it by its Indian name, Maya, if you like) arose that humans themselves produce the ideas, an illusion from which Westerners have still not been able to free themselves. Therefore Aristotle became the "father of the sciences" because he began to construct a human system of philosophy on the bare basis of the internal faculty of thought.

This happened in the Age of Aries, when the sun occupied the astronomical constellation of Aries at the vernal equinox. The new Age (or World Month) made its presence felt by the transfer of the hub of culture from Asia to Europe.

Asia is the cradle of ancient wisdom and religion. In Asia people had preserved the sense and experience of being bound up with the cosmos. They found the latter to be full of gods and elemental beings; they "saw" them, associated with them, and received their teachings and instructions. There was no need for an "argument for the existence of God." The mere suggestion that such a proof might be needed would have sounded ridiculous. The state of affairs is quite different in the

---

[16] This is Bertrand Russell's rendering of the Greek in his *A History of Western Philosophy* (London: George Allen & Unwin Ltd., 1946). Russell adds, "This is interpreted as meaning that *each* man is the measure of all things, and that, when men differ, there is no objective truth in virtue of which one is right and the other wrong. The doctrine is essentially skeptical, and is presumably based on the 'deceitfulness' of the senses." *Tr.*

West, where a culture was developed founded on a form of thinking that has become increasingly divorced from the will and the emotions; thinking that no longer has the run of the cosmos but is penned up in the mind, where indeed it is supposedly produced. When Buddha died, Asia lamented that what it called the "Light of the world" had failed so soon. In a fragment of the poet Ashvaghosha written sometime in the first century A.D. we read:

> The Buddha is the light
> that bears the name "Man."

What has become of that supernatural light that Asia once perceived "out there," and then discovered that it was glowing in the Buddha after he had succeeded in developing his forehead Lotus as he sat under the tree of knowledge? As we have already said, it penetrated humanity. In the Buddha the supernatural light itself still spoke as a man. In Greece it became a shadow of its former self—bare intellectual thought, which became the basis of external science. Just as the cosmic fire sank into kundalini, so in later times there was a limiting of the cosmic light. So there are two distinct stages of knowledge. Whereas Buddha was bringing the third eye in the forehead to a state of supersensual perception, Aristotle turned the divine Ideas into shadowy thought-pictures, exploited by the physical brain to interpret the perceptions of the senses in the outer world. We have here a similar relationship to that of prime[17] and octave in the world of music.

The light of knowledge is not something that remains standing still; it continues effective in the stream of time. The spark of thought that entered Aristotle's soul, has gone on working in science and is not finished yet. The supersensual light that had become man in the Buddha is found 500 years

---

[17] The prime is the lowest note forming an interval in music. *Tr.*

LIVERPOOL
JOHN MOORES UNIVERSITY
AVRIL ROBARTS LRC
TEL. 0151 231 4022

later in Christ Jesus, who said of Himself: "I am the light of the world." (John 8:12). One may rightly say this.

The "I am" is the organ that perceives the light of the world. The physical senses do not see the spiritual light, but the opened faculties of the soul do! In the elements of the earth, in the fire of the burning bush, the Macrocosmic Being revealed Himself to Moses and said of Himself: "I am that I am" (Exodus 3:14). In Egypt "Nuk pu Nuk" was "I am." In India the name Manas was given to that spiritual part of human nature that is capable of recognizing itself as the microcosmic "I am." The gate to the spiritual world, to which the "I am" belongs is the Two-petaled Lotus in the forehead. Its development leads to this realization of "I-am-ness."

Yoga doctrine describes two doors in human beings. The lower door is in the Four-petaled Lotus in the creative depths of the body. This is now shut. What is open to the spiritual world, however, is the upper door in the heights of human consciousness in the head. From this point onward, the student begins to inhale spiritual light. In the body itself there exists the polarity of cosmic fire and cosmic light. It subsists in the tension between willing and thinking, between being and becoming conscious, between sleep and wakefulness. The will is creatively engaged in the processes going on in matter, but in the present era it is not acting alone. We are still very much embedded in natural forces. The more we are able to enter with the light of reason into the dark depths of the substances, will and primal energies of life, the more shall we extend our conquest over the dark kingdom of human individuality. So far, we have conquered only the head region, where the sensory and nerve processes are mainly located. We are masters of ourselves only in the inner light processes of the thoughts. There alone are we wide-awake and human. Incidentally, things are not as the "received wisdom" would have them; namely that everything always has been and always will be, psychosomatically, as it seems to be today. The triumphal march of thought, as it relates to our modern science and philosophy, can be traced by anyone who studies with an unprejudiced mind the spiritual and intellectual history of the last five thousand years.

From the plane that has been reached, we can proceed to bring the regions of life and the energies (of the will) more and more under the control of our own human spirit. This means releasing them from the womb of nature and of the cosmos. The emancipation of human beings from the cosmos is not yet complete. It can not proceed properly without a new spiritual relationship of human beings to the natural kingdom and to the cosmos. Our physical communion with the cosmos must be replaced by a spiritual one. Once again it is time to "lift the serpent."

In the depths of human beings there slumbers the same primeval energy from which the world arose. It is the substance of the creative powers of the cosmic will. The will flows out into desires, it assumes life; basically, the growth processes are those of the will. The energies ascend from the lower into the central regions of the human body, and become rhythmic like the circulation of blood and lymph. Respiration is rhythmic too, although its rhythm is considerably slower than that of the pulse. In the breath, energies are translated from the liquid to the gaseous state (air). Our air is the dwelling-place of light. The governing energies in the warming, nourishing, liquid bloodstream, are conducted to the nerves and sense organs and to the center of inner light. Thought glows between the bloodstream and the path of nervous impulses. Even Galen (ca. A.D. 131–200) distinguishes three regions or systems in the human body which he terms: pneumaphysika, pneumazotikon, and pneumapsychikon—or natural (metabolic) spirit, vital spirit, and psychic spirit.

The stream of energies wells up from below to the floor of the cranium and thus to the physical limits of the human body. In meditation we succeed in getting this process to go even further, to break free from the restraints of the physical and to enter a higher realm, which now lies open to the understanding.

On this point, academics and initiates beg to differ! Followers of Kant consider the borders of knowledge lie where the physical and material basis of the brain leaves off.[18] This will not only be called in question, but the opposite will be experienced by those who make progress in the training. During meditation, the spiritual center of gravity will be displaced from the physical and material foundations of the body in the human aura, and will enter the region of living formative forces beyond the limits of the body!

In figure 7, the Ajna Chakra (see page 88), the reader will note that the section of the spinal column no longer pierces the lotus as it did in the chakras lower down, but passes behind it. This indicates greater freedom than that enjoyed by states of consciousness that are tied to the spine.

Close to the Two-petaled Lotus is a subsidiary Three-petaled Lotus. Yogic doctrine speaks of it as the "knot" in which the three spinal channels finally unite. The olfactory nerve, which ends in 28 fibers, and the optic nerve, which ends in 12 fibers, cooperate. The powers of the Moon (28) and Sun (12) are expressed in these numbers; as, indeed, are Ida and Pingala. According to Steiner, smelling is metamorphosed into synthetic thought, and seeing is metamorphosed into observation. What is more, we meet "higher powers" here—arising out of the change to a body-free state.

In the white circle of the Ajna Chakra, we encounter for the third time the yoni and the lingam, the female, receptive triangle confining the male symbol of procreation. First they

---

[18] According to C.E.M. Joad (*Guide to Philosophy,* London: Victor Gollancz Ltd., 1936) Kant taught that ". . . we know only the world of phenomena, which is the world as it appears, after it has passed through the sieve of our Concepts. The world of noumena, of things as they are independently of us, must remain unknown." Joad criticizes this view. *Tr.*

were red in the Four-petaled Lotus, then golden in the Twelve-petaled Lotus, and now white in the forehead. These are three stages of union (and communion), and each time the procreator bears another name. Each time, too, the part of the body concerned can be compared to some sort of vessel: there is the kettle at the end of the spinal canal, the cup of the heart, and the beaker of the cranium. The pure white disk resembles a wafer. The six centers display the development from red to white, as in the polarity of red rose and white lily.

Vowel number thirteen, *Ong,* is the seed syllable in the white triangle. It is the thirteenth vowel in the cultic sixteen, but twelfth in the usual series. This *O* (*Ong*) is compounded of *A* and *U.* The *O* has no other vehicle or implement than union in the weightless, light spiritual region itself. We no longer have a Divine Pair in the chakra, because it is up to the pupil to achieve union with the divine Atma or spirit.

Communion with the cosmic spirit by the personal spirit is the result of meditation at this stage of development. Only the parturient, divine force itself appears in the guise of the six-faced, three-eyed, six-armed goddess Hakini, sitting on a white lotus. The yogin looks through the six centers and three channels and makes use of these supernatural powers. The goddess (the inner nature of the god) no longer sits above the word, but to one side of it and slightly below it. It is the man or woman who now obtains the divine functions. The Son of Man rules the stars, as John was shown in a symbolic vision (in the Apocalypse).

Above the white triangle we see a sign like the Grail: it is the crescent moon carrying the dark new moon inside it. And thus the spiritual influence of the Sun penetrates the darkness. In the dark moon, the aspirant experiences something of what is meant by "seeing the sun at midnight." The dark area is an expression of the unmanifest sound *M* (*Ma*). It is also called Mahakara. The *M* is forced down into the Moon's sphere by gravity. The crocodile Makara, belonging to the Six-petaled

Lotus, lifts his head out of the waters at the first rays of the Sun, so that it seems to be created from these. Here *Ma* is the sound that gives birth, by its force, to the flow of life, in respect of the suctional force present in the Sun. It is the Laya center of the *M*, the spiritualized *M,* the mother-source of all Maya. The aspirant must pass through this vacuum as if passing through a narrow gateway.

Only on the other side does he or she reach Liberation and the pure kingdom of the spirit that stretches out beyond Manas. The dark area is not only a no-thing, it is less than nothing, just as Rudolf Steiner described the characteristics of the interior of the sun. The fifth part of being is indicated. Kara also means the hand with its five fingers. Makara was the fifth sign of the Indian zodiac: known to us as Capricorn, however. In the head is the student's "land of ice." As the spiritual birth took place at Christmas, at the winter solstice, so the aspirant has a spiritual birth here in the Command Lotus (Ajna Chakra). The yogin becomes spiritually free and master of all that is in his or her body—right down to the forces of the Four-petaled Lotus—becomes master or mistress of the entire colony of beings that are actually within. The light of knowledge shines right down into the depths; the serpent is subdued, the dragon is conquered. The yogin now takes orders from no one else, but only from this union with the cosmic spirit, that is to say from intuition.

From *O* and *M* we get the word *OM,* which is really *AUM,* because the *O* sound is formed from *A* and *U. OM* (*AUM*) is the meditation for this Center, it is its mantra (cf. the word Amen, an old mystery word).

Above the dark area and, so to speak, in the spiritual Sun, is a hook, the "seventeenth finger of the Moon." The sixteen vowels of the Throat Lotus can be thought of as the sixteen fingers or parts (Kala, ages of the moon, sound ether). The seventeenth is "Nirvana-kala," which we could call the primary vowel, though unexpressed. It is a hook, a finger, a flame, and as a mark on paper, part of *A, I, U.* Nirvana is not no-thing; it is a highly active but spiritual state.

In the Western Semitic alphabet, the sign for *Yod* (Greek *Iota*), and for *Vav* or *Vau*, is a hook or finger. Here is the joining of the individual and the cosmic spirit. The hook is a creative primary word, out of which *I, U* and *A* arise. The Egyptians said that the world emanated from the primary word *Wha.*

Where the three spinal channels come together and form the knot, was the top of the staff of Mercury (caduceus) with its two wings, which, when they start to sound and soar, introduce a new Manvantara. The two wings look like the two petals of the lotus, and in varying colors they bear the sound *Ha (Hang)* on the left petal—as seen by the observer—and the combined sound *Ksch (kschang, kscha)* on the right. The word *Hang-scha* means "swan," but also "I am That," I am one with the divinity. In the process of acquiring knowledge, there is a union of the knower with the known spiritually speaking.

The two sounds, which represent the cosmic creative forces on the wings of time, are the subject of meditation. They bear in them the polarity of *H,* the spiritual aspirate, and the mostly earthly sibilant *S,* which has three main variants (*S, Sh, Sch*) and, in this case, the form *X (Ks)*. Although this polarity is otherwise vertical in the body, here it is horizontal, and so we get a cross. Everything has its hour and its destined place! The arousing of the six centers takes place through meditation on the six syllables: Om mani padme hum—O, thou jewel in the lotus! In a hidden way, the six syllables are really seven, because *OM* is properly *AUM* to the Hindus.

There are seven laya centers in our solar cosmos, and seven in the human body, the seven gates of the word, the seven chakras. A laya center is a creative point in which all matter comes to an end, from which it is born and into which it dies. It is the hypomochlion (fulcrum) in which the forces bringing about rest and motion in the balance, form a superordinate (higher ranking) third. Laya is the center of the exhaustion and dissolution of matter. We could call it the mother of things. Every creation springs once more out of the laya condition.

In modern atomic physics, scientists are already theorizing about antimatter, the polar opposite of ordinary matter. According to modern physics, the atom consists of a positive nucleus surrounded by a shell or shells of negatively charged electrons. Antimatter, on the other hand, is postulated as having a negative nucleus with a positive swarm of electrons circling it on the outside.[19]

Decades ago, Steiner spoke of "negative, suctional matter," which could not be conceived of as spatial. He coined the concept of "counterspace," in which even weight or gravity turns into its opposite. In order to understand these things, we must turn away from the physical and material to the Tattwas (etheric formative forces) in living creatures, and thus from the visible to what is open only to supersensual perception! In the above-mentioned meditation formula, "Om mani padme hum," there are subtle processes involved, both for those wishing to experience the rhythmic effect of the familiar sound of the sacred formula, and for those engaging in meditation. Even in sound, the seven syllables correspond to the seven centers. Fairly soon, as they are repeated, we notice a strong vibration in the head that induces changes in consciousness.

The divine worlds are invoked by the syllable *OM,* as are the upper centers. The final syllable *HUM* is used to expel demonic beings. Every time we meditate, there is a danger that demonic forces will ascend from the agitated depths of the psyche or from subhuman elementary levels. The personal "Dweller on the Threshold" is encountered. Whenever any of

---

[19] Brief and interesting accounts of antimatter may be found in the chapter on "Antiparticles" in Martin Gardner's *The Ambidextrous Universe* (London: Pelican Books, 1982), and *The Looking-Glass God,* by Nahum Stiskin (London: The Autumn Press, 1972). The latter examines the concept from an oriental (Japanese and Chinese) point of view. *Tr.*

us strives after the "higher," we expose ourselves to attack from the "lower." This accounts for the tremendous stress laid on moral maturity and moral courage by all the arcane schools.

The following meanings open up to those who meditate on the sacred syllable *OM,* which contains within it the vowels *A-O-U:*

A - The wonder with which, according to an Ancient Greek saying, every philosophy and thus every piece of knowledge begins;

O - A loving embrace, an acceptance of what shines into the spiritual side of nature from the heights;

U - A deliberate descent in the breath into the depths of the body;

M - The stream of breath penetrating the diaphragm and reaching the Navel Lotus or Manipura. A feeling of empathy steals over us in the *M* sound and we find ourselves in unity with it.

In the word *MANI;*

We start from the *M* in the Navel Lotus;

In the following *A,* we grasp at the new, just as a baby does when trying out this sound;

In the *N,* a separation takes place at the periphery of the Navel Lotus;

In the *I,* an extended affirmation opposes the forces thrusting themselves up from below.

In the word *PADME:*

In the *P,* we rest on the firm stronghold of the lotus, from which various forces then gush out;

In the *A,* there is inner taking hold;

In the *D,* there is a downward pressure;

In the *M,* there is empathy with the unknown again;

In the *E,* an intersection maintains itself against various forces.

In the word *HUM:*

In the *H,* there is an explosive blowing away;

In the *U,* there is a determined driving away;

In the *M* is the making of unison.

OM, we are informed, is Bija, the first seed of the Vedas (four primary sacred books of the Hindus). *OM* may also be regarded as the womb, the *Shakti par excellence,* the force being *in* the word.

The two sounds in the Forehead Lotus form the mantra Han-Sa already mentioned. It is nasalized as Hangsa. (Hansa means swan, and symbolizes the white, higher individual soul dwelling in air and light). In meditation it is conducted from the heart to the head. Inspiration accompanies the sound *Hang* (nasalized *Han* or *Ham*), expiration accompanies the sound *Sa.* After the union of the individual soul (Jiva) and the divine spirit (Atma), the yogin remains impassive, and the mantra is reversed into So-ham, meaning "I am That."

H - N - S represents the three regions of the body: *H* is the head; *N* or *M* is the middle of the body centered in the Navel Lotus or Manipura; *S* is the lower region of the fires of desire (the genitals). Such is the mystery of the human being in consonants. In the word Jo-Hannes, we have an expression very similar to the mantra "Hansa." Johannes represents—by his name—men and women and their three regions, reflecting the "three worlds."[20]

Reference has already been made to the connection of the chakras with the endocrine glands. They are all supplied by the vegetative nerves. It would not be correct to equate the chakras with the ganglia or glands; but it is correct to regard them as the superordinate and impelling spirits of the nerves, glands, blood and bones. The nerves and glands are simply manifestations of the chakras on different planes. The endocrine glands in question are:

> the pineal gland (epiphysis),
> the pituitary gland (hypohysis),
> the thyroid gland,
> the adrenal gland,
> the pancreas,
> the gonads (ovaries in women, testicles in the man.
> > The latter develop at the same level as the ovaries,
> > but descend into the scrotum later).

The thymus gland, behind the sternum (breastbone), is closely connected with the endocrines; however, it normally functions to the age of puberty and then retrogrades.

As its position and function indicate the Forehead Lotus is connected with the pituitary gland (hypophysis). The latter

---

[20] The author does not say whether he is referring to John the Baptist, John the Evangelist, or to some other John or Johannes. Johannes is the German form of the Latin Joannes and Greek Iōannēs, which come in turn from the Hebrew Yōchānān. The latter, according to Grimm's "Lexicon Graeco-Latinum," (Leipzig, 1879) means "cui Jehovah propitius est" or "to whom Yahweh is gracious." It will be observed that the final "s" of Johannes was originally an "n." The Greeks changed it to "s"—which matches the "s" in Hansa—but—which does not match—they left out the "ch" or "h" sound. The H-N-S theme first appears in the German (JoHaNNeS) in its entirety. If the John in question was Biblical and not German, this would not count. *Tr.*

holds a central place in the endocrine system, and can be regarded as a sort of switchboard for the whole vegetative nervous system. Its leading position corresponds to the function of the Two-petaled Lotus as an "instruction and command lotus." The activity of other endocrine glands is largely dependent on it. The postpituitary regulates the water-balance (urine) of the body. Pituitary hormones also control growth. In excess they promote gigantism, in deficiency they leave the individual subject to dwarfism. Particularly important is the relationship of the pituitary to the activity of the gonads (sex glands). The functioning of life and consciousness in the human being depends on the balance of hormone production.

What the yogin does is to behave in a feminine way: drawing inward and shutting his house (the external senses) behind him. And here we have revealed to us the secret that the etheric body (vital body) is female in the man and male in the female. This secret dispels many illusions. How can we feel superior to our own etheric body? During meditation on this lotus, the forces that build the body are seen in the spirit. Of the yogin who dies in Ajna consciousness, it is said that he or she becomes one with the Man who was before the three worlds, that is to say with the human prototype as it was before the "fall."

Sound judgment and clear, logical thought are prerequisites for the development of the Forehead Lotus. By distinguishing truth from the Maya of mere appearance, a focal point and center of gravity is created in the brow. Correct meditation is the key to success in this. The conceptions that are placed before the mind's eye must be brought from within the soul, not from the outside world. By constant practice, we learn to turn the formative-force body every way.

Gradually, the etheric currents intertwine like a network to form a sort of mesh on the surface of the etheric body. This thin "skin" must, above all, be permeable to all the various currents impinging on it. This makes perception possible. Enclosing ourselves in an integument is a Saturnian function. The network has an inner relationship with the Two-thousand-petaled Lotus, which has to be opened from within by each individual. That points us to the future.

A current comes from the Sixteen-petaled Lotus that fashions rounded forms in the Two-petaled Lotus. From the mid-point of this current in the Two-petaled Lotus, streams flow along the two hands. They move the etheric body. The higher ego is born, it is free, and communicates with the spiritual world. The Forehead Lotus is the gateway to the spirit.

Our last three verses can now be allowed to speak for themselves so that the reader may respond to their message:

Verse 36

When the yogi closes the house
which hangs without support,
the knowledge whereof he has gained
by the service of Parama-guru,
and when the Cetas by repeated practice
becomes dissolved in this place
which is the abode of uninterrupted bliss,
he then sees within the middle of
and in the space above (the triangle)
sparks of fire distinctly shining.

Verse 37

He then also sees the Light
which is in the form of a flaming lamp.
It is lustrous like the clearly shining morning sun,
and glows between the Sky and the Earth.
It is here that the Bhagavan manifests Himself
in the fullness of His might.
He knows no decay,
and witnesseth all,
and is here as He is in the region
of Fire, Moon, and Sun.

Verse 38

This is the incomparable and delightful
abode of Vishnu.

The excellent Yogi at the time of death
joyfully places his vital breath (Prana)
here and enters (after death)
that Supreme, Eternal, Birthless,
Primeval Deva, the Purusa,
who was before the three worlds,
and who is known by the Vedanta.[21]

---

[21] Arthur Avalon, *The Serpent Power,* pp. 404, 407, 411.

The Thousand-Petaled Lotus

Underneath the optic thalamus belonging to the cerebrum lies the diencephalon (interbrain), which is the supreme authority over the autonomic nerves. Body temperature, cell metabolism, and pulse rate are all regulated by it. The pituitary (below) and the pineal gland (above), both belong to the Command Lotus and look like small protrusions. They are in a relationship of polar tension to one another. The pineal gland belongs to the region of the Thousand-petaled Lotus, the Sahasrara Chakra; which, from its position in the head, is also called the crown chakra or the 7th chakra. Yogic doctrine states that Sahasrara is at the end of the middle spinal current (sushumna). The current has a fire nature; it is Saturnian and runs up to this particular center below the crown of the head. In contrast to the other chakras, the petals of this chakra tend to droop or hang down, even when consciousness is given to it. (See figure 8 on page 108.)

The tonsure of the monks apparently has to do with the external patch in the middle of the center. The patterning suggests that this circular patch is a point of attachment to the superior divine world. The divine will creates pictures in light, which later become reality. The world can be regarded as the shape given to the divine imagination.

Figure 8. Sahasrara chakra, the Thousand-petaled Lotus.

It is conceivable that, in the remote past, the lobes of the brain were tongues of fire. Only when the body solidified into something physical did they congeal and become locked away in a bony cranium. In babies, the fontanelles remain open for a little while after birth.

According to the secret doctrine of various schools, the pineal gland is an atrophied light-organ, the remains of a human third eye (the parietal eye). It used to stick out above the head but was brought inside it when the brain lobes were "boxed up." It is now the size of a cherry, and it awaits its resurrection.

Shape-building forces emanate from this center. Its influence on the gonads can affect reproduction: when the influence is faulty, degeneracy occurs. Even today, the pineal gland separates calcium salts such as are needed for the formation of the bones. This has been called "brain sand," something necessary for our thought processes.

The Thousand-petaled and Two-petaled Chakras go together in their polarity like heat and light, willing and thinking. Their cooperation produces the prototypes for the physical development of human beings.

During my life, I have met many people who frequently see visions over which they have no control. Images and snatches of poetry haunt them in a pathological way. There is little that can be done for them and they are treated as abnormal. When I have asked, in such cases, whether they had ever suffered a severe blow on the back of the head, perhaps in a fall, I have invariably received an affirmative answer. To me, this indicates that the pineal gland has been injured. But what can happen by accident to often very ordinary people can also be produced during meditation on this center in a healthy and self-controlled way.

Interestingly enough, the pineal occupies a very significant position in the head: it lies in the golden section![22] What is

---

[22] For interesting reading on the golden section, see H. E. Huntley's *The Divine Proportion*, (New York: Dover Publications, 1970). *Tr.*

more, it is opposite the static pole of the Root-Support Lotus. The center of memory is at the back of the head. Memory and love are the polar roots of human speech; so it is understandable why the texts say that "the yogin who has gained a footing in the Forehead Lotus holds the lotus that is above him (the crown chakra), with all the powers of speech, in the palm of his hand."

This center, where the fires of the lower desires are wholly spiritualized, contains the highest seat of the divine in man or woman, and holds the spiritual essence that underlies existence. It is where, for the first time, the aspirant is set free from all illusion. An even higher degree of freedom is attained here than in the Two-petaled Lotus. The yogin who could maintain consciousness in the Two-petaled Lotus would be under the direct gaze of the highest cosmic power of the word that created the world and the things in it. The power of speech would then be in his or her spiritual hand.

The sound M in the Eye Lotus is the androgyne. In the Thousand-petaled Lotus, the 50 letters are repeated twenty times. Mankind is the tenth member of the hierarchies; and, as male and female, we are "20." Twenty also means the Sun. In the Orient, there was a god "20," the Sun-god, and a god "30," who was Sin, the Moon Spirit. Therefore Sun plus Moon make 50—or the Sanskrit alphabet of 50 letters. After multiplication by twenty, so that the entire person becomes solar, the letters are distributed among the thousand petals of the lotus. The Crown Lotus is therefore by way of being a generative organ of the gods. It was closed from outside when the gods withdrew. From inside, from the individual outward, this roof of the world has to be opened. The three spinal channels are etherealized here into a threefold H-sound. It is the creativity of the still unmanifest H, named Hakara as the lowest of the three H's.

The two others are the Visarga-sound. However, there it is only what forms this sound, that is to say, S without a vowel—the *S* that is converted into the *H*. The sound change from *H* to *S* is well known. It happened on the way from spirit to matter. Here the reverse takes place. The materialized sound *S* is dematerialized back into *H*. And the thing that is formed on the return journey, the thing that from *S* becomes *H* again, represents "practice," the *prima materia* and is connected with the highest part of humans: the spiritual being or Atma. The twofold root of the *prima materia:* one branch going to the man, the other to his wife—and that is the Materia!—man and earth. . .

In the three *H* sounds, two of which are *S* sounds in transition to the *H,* the yogin sees Brahma, the spirit god, Vishnu the progeny, and the "I-myself" of the human being— both the divinity as self and the reflection of that divinity, the human ego.

This region is where the fire of Shiva works, disperses and etherealizes. Yoga shows how all sounds dissolve into one another and are converted into the Laya state. Shiva is in the Hakara. His paradise-mountain, Kailasa, is also the human cranium. *H* and *S* (Hansa) represent the union of consciousness and matter, humanity and earth, spirit and nature, Purusha and Prakriti.

The sounds merge into one another like this: *Kscha* into *La, La* into *Ha, Ha* into *Sa, Sa* into *Sha,* and so on until *A* is reached. When the sounds are dissolved, the centers dissolve into their point of origin and this dissolves into the general world consciousness. What is depicted here is a sort of "struggle of all against all" on a higher plane. The periphery is sucked into the center. The Maya of plurality disappears. The Thousand-petaled Lotus is also depicted as Baldachin, from which the reddish nectar drops down. All other lotuses recur in it. Thus the Twelve-petaled Lotus is in its exact center.

In meditation the yogin finds himself or herself. He or she finds the "island of jewels" in the head. We are reminded here of the amber-like quadrigeminal plate inside the cranium. The dissection of corpses was strictly forbidden in the Middle Ages and was punishable by death. But the inner sight of the yogins enabled them to know the internal arrangements of the human body. Alternatively, it is possible that the talk of "jewels" is a piece of imagery, a metaphor for crystal-clear thought. Also there may be a reference to the gem-decked altar of the Heart Lotus.

As mentioned above, the other lotuses recur in the head. Trunk chakras invariably have their polar opposites in the head, by which they are controlled. The more the power of pure, crystal-clear thought is developed—and this is essential for directing our affairs—the more influence will be invested in the upper light pole, and generations of depravity coursing through our veins will be brought under control.

It must be obvious by now that there are two polar currents (they meet at spiritual infinity). One of them flows upward from the Root Lotus, although the blood flows downward from the heart. The stream that flows upward in and around the spine is not material, but is a powerful stream of creative energies. These are not yet fully under the control of most individuals, even though they emerge from the physical.

The Hindus refer these creative energies to Rudra-Shiva, lord of the physical. We must not take the name literally, but it will help us to a better understanding. We could, of course, employ modern terminology, but there would hardly be any advantage in doing so.

The other stream flows from the upper pole of inner light which creates order and knowledge. It comes from the region of the spirit-god known to the Hindus as Brahma.

The one stream comes from the pole of being, the other from the pole of consciousness, and they meet in the heart in a go-between, the balancing and healing god Vishnu. They unite in a higher power of love ("fire," heat) and in the inner light of the heart springing from wise understanding. The stream rising up from below used to be known as the "fig-tree." Chavvah (Eve), the mother of all living—which is what her name means—wore a fig leaf. Christ cursed the barren fig-tree to remain fruitless. This indicates to us that the atavistic old abilities of the lower forces are exhausted.

Why? Because human aspirations are tainted with evil. Moral evil was ingested by mankind in the distant past, but we were not originally evil. The tragedy was brought about by the power of the Adversary, opposer of the creation of mankind; and what was once a pure being became pervaded by the forces of darkness. The original human image was defaced. Invading antagonistic influences became naturalized and were handed down by heredity, being transmitted in the blood line from generation to generation. This became the curse. The Adversary of the true, light-pure human being is to blame. So what is needed is for the Old Adam to be made new in the spirit of moral goodness.

People's feet carry them on their various errands in response to the will. Thus the sacred ceremony of feet-washing by Christ points us to our need of cleansing and sanctification "from the ground up."

Some members of the human race have been able to develop the power of pure thought. This is completely objective and free from sympathy and antipathy. It is thinking that leads to total abstraction and the emptying of consciousness, and this is mentioned in our verses. The void, or nothing, is not the final stage however.[23] It is transitional—a threshold experience. Today, humanity faces this void. But on its other side, thinking changes into higher perceptions in a sort of resurrection from the dead. And higher perceptions produce higher abilities. This

---

[23] It is interesting to compare these ideas concerning pure thought and "nothing," with what the Hegelian philosopher, Francis Sedlák has to say in his book *Pure Thought and the Riddle of the Universe*, (London: George Allen & Unwin, 1919): "In answer to the question, How to initiate the system of pure thought? we must say: By thinking either pure Nothing or pure Being. . . . the beginning is made by thinking Being—Nothing—Being . . . ." *Tr.*

resurrected thinking has a center of gravity that has been shifted from the logical reasoning built up in the brain, and has been placed in a living realm which is free from the body. It becomes a creative spiritual experience, free from physical foundations. As I have already mentioned, purified feeling and willing must be combined with the living idea. In this way we are enabled to create a higher being for ourselves, like a sort of Baron Munchausen, who pulled himself out of a swamp by his own hair.[24]

Finally, let me picture this possible process once more for readers, for it is the beginning and end of all efforts made in the direction of healthy evolution. We have to realize that, in ancient yoga, the development of pure thought in the head chakras was the real aim. "Nectar and ambrosia" were the heavenly food sought by the yogin. In our own day and age, the pivotal point, or inner solstice for this development has been reached for all.

The verses describe how, in meditation, the yogin dis-covers the "Guru's Throne" in a "Mountain of Silver." In the Ancient Wisdom, the head was an inner Moon region. Silver belonged to it in its fluid condition and highest potentization.

In meditation, the yogin comes through the upper chakras to the great Moon adept, whose feet stand in the human head. By using the ability gained by completely pure thought, the yogin touches—with the highest capacity of his or her soul— the lowest part (the feet) of the divinity. We have already seen how the feet are a symbol of the will. Here, then, the yogin begins to discover something of the will of the godhead—not simply suffering it, but consenting to it. This is the start of spiritual fruitfulness in the ethereal sphere outside the body. What has been initiated there is then lead below into the Heart Lotus, the sphere of the inner altar, of inner devotion, of the

---

[24] "Munchausen" (The baron), a German hero of most marvelous adventures. *Tr.*

inner ever-burning lamp, and also of the breath of prayer and self-sacrifice.

Modern people cannot do without the development of the lotuses. We understand how important is the cultivation of the Heart Lotus, the sphere of the "Son." This helps us resist the temptation to turn our backs on the world at the wrong time in order to find deliverance for ourselves while leaving behind our brothers and sisters. In the reception of the spiritual cosmic seed lie opportunities not only for perceiving our own incarnations, the paths of the soul and of the spirit in their interplay between spiritual, cosmic and earthly spheres, but also the great secrets of world evolution—all of which find entry through the upper gateway of mankind, where it is possible to catch a glimpse of the divine.

We need to cultivate the chakras. This is managed first of all by meditation. For this to succeed, there has to be inner change (without detriment to external obligations), as required by the internal necessity of the stages of the path that have been described. Meditation is the "Holy of Holies" of yoga; everything else simply leads up to it. We need a higher power in order to have something to counteract the disintegrating influences of our own civilization and disruptive intellect. In the battle against moral evil which rages round us every step of the way, we need help from a world of moral goodness, that is to say, from the world of the spirit. The power and peace of this world revives and heals our injured life-functions. This power and peace can be obtained by constantly repeated, rhythmic meditation through the chakras, because they are the gates through which the realm of the cosmic forces intervenes.

Glossary

Agni: fire, god of sacrifice.

akasha: the pure sound ether.

Ajna chakra: the Two-petaled Lotus, also known as the sixth chakra or the third eye.

anahata: the foundation of the cosmic word.

Anahata chakra: the heart or fourth chakra, which is also known as the Twelve-petaled Lotus.

arupa: the stage of no-form.

asana: the third stage of yoga development, instruction or posture.

Atman: the individual soul or life force.

bindu: the creative dot out of which the Word proceeds, a drop, as of semen.

bo tree: the tree of knowledge.

buddhi: understanding, intellect, imagination, faculty of discrimination. An aspect of mental life, the buddhi is the faculty of judgment and imagination that gives rise to intellectual beliefs and makes understanding possible.

chakra: the seven vital powers.

chela: student.

chitrini: an imperceptible channel of energy in the central canal in the spine.

devis: (Devas) gods and goddesses; the highest incarnations of the six worlds of existence.

dharana: concentration, the sixth stage of yoga development.

dhyana: the seventh stage of yoga development; it is stage two of the three-part process of meditation; meditative study of both the unchanged noumenon and changing phenomena.

gunas: quality of the psychic life.

guru: a teacher, "Bringer of Light."

hamsa: (Han-Sa, or Hansa, or Hangsa) a mythical bird, a goose or a gander; also translated as swan. The bird is both aquatic and atmospheric which may be analogous to the soul which wanders to and fro in this world and the next, or, as the immortal self.

ida: the feminine secondary psychic channel along the spine, associated with the moon.

Ishvari: another name for the Goddess Kundalini.

Kailasa: paradise mountain, the cranium.

kundalini: used in Tantric forms of Indian meditation to connote the latent power awakened in the meditation process. From the lowest chakra, kundalini moves upward until it unites with the thousand-petaled center, causing *Samadhi.*

Kundalini Yoga: a reuniting of the Goddess Kundalini, the eternal feminine, with the eternal masculine, Shiva, the begetter of the physical world.

laya center: a creative point where all matter comes to an end from which it is born and into which it dies.

lingham: Shiva's phallus, symbol of procreation.

manas: mind, the "I am." The manas or "sense of mind," is another aspect of mental life. It is the instrument which assimilates and synthesizes sense impressions and brings the self into contact with external objects. It lacks discrimination and furnishes the self only with precepts which must be transformed and acted upon by a higher mental function, the buddhi.

Maya: goddess of illusion.

Merv: a mythical Indian mountain. The "inner" merv refers to the spinal column.

mudras: a symbolic gesture in dance, ritual, tantric meditation or iconography, especially gestures of the hand and fingers.

Muladhara chakra: the first chakra located at the origin of the spine, also known as the root chakra and the Four-petaled Lotus.

nadis: psychic nerves. A subtle pathway of psychic energy in the body-mind, (Nada).

niyama: the second stage of yoga development. The search for inner and outer purity.

Patanjali: teacher of Kundalini yoga practice.

pingala: the masculine secondary channel of psychic energy along the spine, associated with the sun.

prakiti: original source; nature; lower condition.

Prana: life force.

pranayama: the fourth stage of yoga development, control of breath.

pratyahara: the fifth stage of yoga development, conscious mastery of the senses.

Prithivi: a Hindu goddess personifying the earth, life ether, the cause of solidity.

purusha: spiritual vision, higher condition.

rajas: passion.

rupa: the world of abstract form; denotes corporeality in the distinction between mind and body. The physical form related to the five sense organs.

sahasrara: the upper brain; relating to the sixth chakra, sometimes identified with the pineal gland.

Sahasrara chakra: the Thousand-petaled Lotus which is also called the crown or the seventh chakra.

samadhi: the eighth stage of yoga development, literally "union with the Lord," a profound state of meditation that is synonymous with enlightenment.

sattwa: light, wisdom, truth.

Shiva: lord of all creatures, who has a three-fold nature—creator, destroyer and preserver.

sushumna: the primary of the central psychic channels along the spine in which kundalini arises.

Surya: the sun god.

Svadhisthana chakra: the second chakra located at the root of the genitals. Also known as the Six-petaled Lotus.

tamas: darkness or apathy; one of the three gunas.

tattwas: etheric formative forces.

vajrini: a channel of energy that makes up the shusumna.

vedas: refers to an entire corpus of literature extending from the *Rig Veda* to the *Upanishads,* extending to later works such as the *Sutras.* The Vedas transmit the ancient revelations in a series of hymns, ritual texts and speculations composed over a period of a millenium beginning *ca* 1400 B.C.

Vishuddha chakra: the Sixteen-petaled Lotus, also known as the throat or fifth chakra.

Yama: from the *Rig Veda,* god of death who instructs in the first stages of yoga development.

yoga: literally, a harness; to study yoga means that one turns the physical vehicle into a spiritual temple.

yoni: the female receptive triangle.

Index

Werner Bohm was born in 1896. He was interested in pursuing a career in medicine but was prevented from doing so by the outbreak of World War I. After the war, he married and became a director of a major company, while continuing to explore his interest in alternative medicine, Hindu philosophy and astrology. After his discovery of the works of Rudolf Steiner and Dr. von Veltheim-Ostrau, Werner Bohm became convinced of the need for this book on the chakras. He died in 1959.